Gentleman Cadet to Headmaster

The Author

Lieut.Colonel A.E.G. Haig M.C.

Gentleman Cadet
to Headmaster
Two rewarding careers

The Pentland Press Ltd.,
EDINBURGH

© A.E.G. Haig 1988
First published in 1988 by
The Pentland Press Limited,
Kippielaw, Haddington,
East Lothian, Scotland.

Typeset by Print Origination (NW) Ltd.,
Printed and bound by Holmes McDougall Ltd.,
Edinburgh
Jacket Design by Ann Ross Paterson

ISBN 0 94627 63 5

To my darling wife Joane.
who has been a wonderful
help to me through good times
and bad.

Contents

AUTHOR'S PREFACE

Not for the first time, I am following the example of my more distinguished father. He, when he retired, wrote his memoirs primarily for the benefit of his immediate family and in particular for the interest of his grandchildren.

His manuscript has been of enthralling interest to me. Above all I enjoyed reading about his early life.

So I wrote this book for my grandchildren and consequently wrote at some length on my childhood.

I wrote it for the same very limited number of readers. I persuaded some of my golfing friends to read through my manuscript. They were very polite and advised me that they thought it deserved a wider distribution.

So here it is. I hope you may be amused and interested by it.

A. Haig
Bexhill-on-Sea
August, 1988

Childhood and Preparatory School

I was born at No. 4 West Ridge Road Rawalpindi on the North West Frontier Province of India, on 24th February 1912. My father was then Adjutant of a Mountain Brigade. My mother took me to England when I was seven months old. I am told that on our arrival in England I was in pretty poor shape and yellow with jaundice.

Malcolm and I spent the next two or three years in Granny Haig's house in Kensington Park Gardens. I cannot remember my grandmother at all. In fact my only memory of 'K.P.G.' was one day when I was looking out of the nursery window, when I saw one of Granny's coachmen leading away one of the carriage horses. I asked Nanny where he was going and she answered 'To the zoo'. Many months later Nanny took Malcolm and me to the zoo for a treat; I asked if we could go and see the horse, whose name I had forgotten. Eventually Nanny had to admit to me that the reason he had been taken to the zoo was to go to the slaughterhouse to become food for the lions! I was horrified.

My parents returned from India in October 1914 and soon afterwards my mother rented 42 Dorset Road at Bexhill, where we spent the whole war period, punctuated by frequent visits to Granny Bromwich at Chenistone, a fine Georgian house in Tilford Road, Farnham. It was at these two houses that my very happy childhood began. I loved my mother dearly and I was blessed by having the very best possible elder brother. Malcolm, although five years older than me, was a wonderful companion and fortunately never seemed to tire of my company. While at Chenistone we saw a lot of my Aunt Alice and my cousins the Powells (Hilda, Elsie, Molly and Nancy) and the Raitts (Margaret and Frances) and so Malcolm and I, of the grandchildren, were outnumbered six to two by the female sex.

I remember throwing acorns at convoys of lorries taking German prisoners to their camp, and playing war games, in which Lintot, the gardener, was always the Hun. I learnt to ride a bicycle there and had my first ride in a car. Granny had a Ford sedan and I well remember when we reached the speed of 30 m.p.h. on the way to Windsor.

My father very infrequently came home on two or three days leave. I was very proud of him, but really did not get to know him until I was almost seven years old.

Our main pastimes at this period were stamp-collecting, playing with lead soldiers, playing with cigarette cards, cricket on the lawn, archery, and bicycling. At Farnham I used to be allowed once a week to help the Powells with their stall in Castle Road, collecting vegetables for the Navy. I can remember being saddened by the news of Lord Kitchener's death and thrilled by the news of my Uncle Arthur's escape from a Turkish prison; curiously enough the mother of another member of his escaping party lived a few doors away from us in Dorset Road. Malcolm went to school at Elstree Lodge, Bexhill, in 1916, and the next year I started my education at a kindergarten in Sea Road, run by Miss O'Sulivan.

Dad did not return from the war until 1919. By then, he was the youngest Brevet Lieutenant Colonel in the Royal Artillery, had been awarded a CMG and a DSO and had been mentioned in despatches no fewer than seven times. He was given command of the Depot Regiment at Fort Brockhurst, between Gosport and Fareham. This was the first time that the family had been together. The four of us used to go for long bicycle rides. Dad played golf at Lee-on-the-Solent and Malcolm and I started playing there. We all thoroughly enjoyed going over Portsmouth harbour on the ferry, seeing the battleships, cruisers, destroyers and so on, and the piquet boats with their shining brass funnels taking senior officers from one ship to another. It was always assumed that Malcolm and I would both go into the Army, but at this period I announced that I thought I would rather go into the Royal Marines. Shortly afterwards, however, Dad and I were going in to Portsmouth and when we got to the Hard, a ferry was preparing to cast off. Dad seized my hand and we ran to the ferry and jumped on as it was moving off. I landed in a heap on the deck. After a moment I said to Dad, 'Do Marines often have to do that?' to which he answered 'Constantly', and that was the end of my rebellion!

Fort Brockhurst covered a large area and was completely surrounded by a moat. The perimeter buildings were all of one storey and were surmounted by earth and grass. There were ducks and swans on the moat. Our kitchen garden was on the roof, where also blackberries grew. We had a punt for our own use, a tennis court and stables. My father's groom gave us our first riding lessons, and when Malcolm was away at school he used to take me to watch football and cricket matches. I went by tram daily in term-time to Fareham, where I shared a governess with David Wilkinson. I remember getting the second prize! Another great pleasure was being taken to the Garrison Church and trying not to giggle when one or two of the trumpeters (whom I envied greatly) tried to make me laugh. After the service Dad led the parade back to the Fort, riding Daisy and followed by two mounted trumpeters. Once or twice, I was taken to the Troop's concerts, which I enjoyed greatly. They were great days, especially when Malcolm was at home. It was here that we started to build up a fine collection of gramophone records. It was here also that Dick was born in 1920. It was at this time that, at last, I got to know and appreciate my father. My love for him was tinged with a shade of fear as I had soon discovered that he had a quickish temper. If ever he got angry with Malcolm, I used, tactlessly, to stick up for my brother over-zealously which, of course, made the whole thing worse.

Unfortunately we left Fort Brockhurst before the end of 1920. Elstree Lodge had by then moved to larger premises in Hastings and was now called Sandrock Hall. I joined the school for the summer term of 1920 which was also Malcolm's last term there. He was head boy. Much to his credit he managed to keep an older brother's eye on me without prejudicing his responsibilities as head boy, and of course his presence made it so much easier for me to adapt to the life of a 'boarder'.

The headmaster was a clergyman: G.A. Scott, (Gas). He had been a Cambridge cricket Blue. He suffered very badly from tuberculosis and, sadly, died soon after I left the school. He claimed to have been the true inventor of the googly, but as he was a fast bowler, passed his invention on to Bosanquet, who has always been credited with being its inventor. Judging by my first letter home, I must have been a conceited little 'pipsqueak' as an extract reads: 'I played in jun game. I made top score and then bawled and cort all the rest out'! My mother and Dick had gone to live at Chenistone; my father was back in India. Malcolm went to Winchester in September 1920.

I enjoyed my time at Sandrock Hall. There were over sixty boys there, all boarders. Mrs Scott was extremely nice and the three

Sandrock Hall 1920
Seated in the middle of the group left to right:- Mrs Scott: Rev. G.A. Scott:
the Author's brother Malcolm: on the ground at Malcolm's feet is the Author

daughters too. One of the more senior boys was a very gifted story teller and used to delight the whole dormitory after 'lights out' with his exciting stories. The other thing I remember about him was that he suffered terribly from chilblains. His name was Gino Watkins. Within six years of leaving Sandrock he had become a famous Arctic explorer and three years later he was killed when leading an expedition, as a result of a kayak accident. Another boy who became very well known was Richard Murdoch, the comedian.

I gradually climbed up the school. I had three years in the cricket first eleven and two seasons in the soccer eleven and the rugby fifteen. My last year I was captain of cricket. One of the schools against which we played matches was Summer Fields in St. Leonards. When visiting them we used to travel on a privately hired tram. We enjoyed these matches particularly, as Summer Fields always seemed to have a large number of titled boys in their teams and on the tram going home we were full of such quips as 'I was marked by a marquis' or 'I caught a count' or 'I bowled a baron'. On my last visit there I must have done something special because I was presented with a peacock's feather, which was proudly waved on the top deck of our tram on the way back.

The holidays we spent at Chenistone, bicycling, golfing at Hankley, playing cricket and croquet, and picnicking with the Powell family. We lived in great luxury. The day always started with family prayers in the dining room, taken by my Granny, who seemed permanently to wear a 'poke' bonnet, and attended by the whole family, the indoor staff and the sealyhams Taffy and Bunty. Bunty was rather apt to get under the table and give my slippers or my shorts a playful nip, so I was quite pleased when all dogs had to wear muzzles during a rabies scare. After prayers we helped ourselves from entrée dishes on the sideboard to huge and delicious breakfasts.

Happy as we were at Chenistone, we were all delighted when Dad came home on leave in 1922. He rented a cottage for us on Fareham Quay with only the road between us and the water. We had the use of Mr Grigg's boat and played golf at Lee-on-the-Solent. Then we were delighted to hear that Dad, to avoid having another three or four years in India, was going to retire from the Army. It was during this period that I watched first class cricket for the first time. At Portsmouth we saw the first post-war Australian team play. Their side included J.M. Gregory, Warwick Armstrong, Macartney, and

Ryder, to name a few. Mr Scott used to take the first and second elevens to the County ground in Hastings one day each year. A.E.R. Gilligan, who later captained England, was my hero. Little did I know then that he was destined to become a friend of mine forty years later.

We moved to The Croft at Frindsbury soon after my father had taken up his job as secretary of the Sapper HQ Officers Mess at Chatham. It made a wonderful home for the family. It was a big house with a large garden which included an excellent tennis court, a 'cricket lawn', a large kitchen garden, and ample space for chickens. We had a whole time gardener whose wage was £1 per week! (I have just engaged a young gardener for 3 hours per week for £2.75 per hour (1984)!)

Soon after we moved in, my father bought the family's first car, a 'round nosed' Morris Cowley tourer; despite this my father normally used to bicycle the 3½ miles to Brompton Barracks. I well remember him arriving back for lunch one day, very hot and exhausted. When he had recovered his breath he explained, 'a bloody butcher's boy tried to pass me on Frindsbury Hill'. Until the end of his days he always drove a car rather like riding a horse; when accelerating he used to urge the car on with his buttocks. It was an exciting life for us boys. Malcolm and I used to go to Brompton Barracks for riding lessons from the Sapper 'rough riders'. My father came to watch one of our early lessons and afterwards congratulated Malcolm on his good seat. I said 'How did I do, Dad?' I was rather hurt when he answered 'You rode like a pea on a drum.' I must admit that the first time we cantered without stirrups, I fell off at the corners quite frequently.

We had tremendous children's parties. The Sappers, the Royal Navy and the Marines vied with each other as to which of their Messes gave the best parties. We went to a lot of 'thé dansants' which I did not enjoy much. One had one's own dance programme, and if one did not book fully one had either to go to the aid of a 'wallflower' or else to lock oneself in the lavatory. I generally followed the latter course.

We went out beagling with the RE pack. We biked out to Rochester and Cobham Park Golf Club (about five miles away). We played a lot of tennis both at home and at the Officers' Combined Services Recreation Club. The Club organised a very good children's tennis tournament at which I won my first individual prize. We all became very keen film goers—silent black and white films of course. My favourites were Charlie Chaplin, Harold Lloyd and Buster Keaton of the comics, Tom Mix in cowboy films; Rudolph Valentino, Ronald Colman, the Barrymores, the Gish sisters, Wallace Berry and many others in dramas, of which 'Blood and Sand', 'The Four Horsemen of the Apocalypse' and 'The Four Feathers' remain vividly in my memory.

In the summer holidays after leaving Sandrock Hall, I was lucky enough to be chosen to play cricket for the Preparatory Schools against the London Elementary Schools at Lords. My mother took me up to London—Malcolm had just gone off to the RMA Woolwich. It was a dull match, but a great experience. I managed to take one wicket and was about 7 not out when we won the match. I made the mistake of watching our innings from a top balcony of the pavilion and this, combined with another error—putting my batting gloves on before taking off my blazer—caused me a nightmarish experience. When the wicket fell which required me to go in to bat, I leapt up and struggled to get my blazer off without removing my batting gloves. This proved impossible. By the time I was organised I was in an awful flap. I dashed down the staircase where on the first floor I was confronted by a stuffed bear which I was sure had not been there when I went up! I looked for another staircase without success and so continued my descent. I emerged from the pavilion by quite the wrong door, wondering whether the umpires would rule me out under the two minute rule, only to find that the incoming batsman had only just reached the pavilion.

2

Winchester

My father drove me down to Winchester for the start of Short Half (the Christmas term) 1925. To my relief I had passed the entrance examination and was placed in JP 2 (the lowest form). Malcolm had left the school two terms before my arrival. He had coached me thoroughly in the quaint Winchester language and in such matters as the colours of the different houses and the names of the housemasters. For a year or more we had called a lavatory a foricas, and so on, so the dreaded 'Notions Examina' after the first fortnight held no terrors for me. I only made one mistake. I was asked 'What is your crack?' I blushed scarlet and answered 'The slit in my bottom' which is the term we used at Sandrock for that part of one's anatomy. The prefects all roared with laughter—the correct answer was 'the space between my bed and my chest of drawers'.

I was promoted to JP 1 for my second term but got stuck in that form for four terms, which was very bad. After two terms in MP 3 without getting promotion, Dad gave me a very strong 'talking-to', including a threat that if I did no better the next term he would take me away from Winchester and send me to Kings School, Rochester. I vividly remember in one report my French Don merely put 'Knows no French'; this galled me as the only prize I had won at Sandrock was one for French! All this coincided with a change of housemaster. The very colourless, uncaring, housemaster we had had was replaced by Harry Altham, a Hampshire cricketer and a desperately keen 'pot hunter'. The previous housemaster was a bachelor; Harry had a charming wife. As a result of all this I achieved two consecutive 'removes' and thereby got into the 'Army class' at the correct time.

When I joined the House (Furley's) we suffered from a distinct lack of any gifted games players amongst our senior 'men'. I got in to the House cricket eleven in my first summer term and can boast that I played in every House match during the five years I was there. My very first House match was against the house which provided the school wicket-keeper. He was a huge ginger-haired man, about 6ft 2in, who must have weighed well over twelve stone. As I took guard, the monster behind the stumps kindly pointed out that one of my bootlaces was undone and advised me to do it up.

I said 'Yes, sir,' but I was all fingers and thumbs and he said 'Can I help you?'

'No, thank you, sir,' I answered, 'I've done it now, sir.'

'Don't call me sir,' he said, 'My name's Bonham-Carter.'

'Oh, sorry, s-' (I checked myself) 'Bonham-Carter.' By the time he had crouched behind the stumps I felt about three feet tall!

Another match we played later the same term was against Kingsley's house. He was captain of Lords and had just recently made a century against Eton. We were playing in Meads and the playing area included the beautiful tall plane trees. Kingsley had made his 100 when I was put on to bowl. He treated my first two balls with respect, but the next one he hit high up into the branches of the tallest tree, Our captain got underneath it, watched it drop from branch to branch like a pinball and eventually caught it. My letter home reported, 'We played against Kingsley's house yesterday, I got him out third ball.'

My cricket at Winchester was very disappointing. I failed to get into Lords (the first eleven). I had a good chance of doing so in my last term, but unfortunately the Army examination coincided with the two days of the Eton match. Harry warned me early on that as Davies Scourfield, our best batsman, was also taking the Army exam and would have to have a substitute during exam times and bat when he could, he thought that it would be too disrupting to have me in the eleven as well. My highlight was playing for Hampshire Club & Ground (County second eleven) against Lords: I had been having nets at Southampton in the Easter holidays with the young pros. I think Harry must have told the County that he would be very grateful if I could be included in their team for this match. I made 43, which launched me into a long overdue improvement.

We became the outstanding house in competitions. Alan Young and Roger Winlaw were our stars. We won the cricket and soccer cups in both my last two years, the senior steeplechase, when we had five of the first ten to finish, (I was ninth), the drill cup, in which I was platoon sergeant, and all the gymna cups.

Quite early on I got keen on gymna, largely because my cousin

John was very good at it. The annual individual competition was for the Headmaster's medals. In my penultimate year, thinking I had no chance of winning a medal, I was very relaxed. John tied with another man for the gold, and I was fourth. The 'powers that be', including the headmaster, went into a huddle, and decided that John and Post should each get a gold medal, the third man got the silver, and so I won the bronze. My last year I was favourite to win the gold, but I was beaten by one point, and so got the silver. I have often wondered whether my keenness on gym was a factor in my lack of improvement in cricket, whether it made me muscle-bound at the wrong time in my development; I just do not know.

The first beating I received was during my first half when I was 'library cad', which involved keeping the prefects' library clean, preparing their Sunday tea party, and so on. We were beaten with ground-ash sticks which were cut and kept in a vase in the library which had to be kept filled with water. I failed to top-up the vase with water and so was beaten. Juniors were beaten on the bottom, three-year men on the back. This was stopped when Harry took over and the cane took over from the ground ash. He also stopped another dangerous custom. If a three-year man thought a junior man had offended him, he was empowered to order him to 'sport a hole', which demanded that the junior should bend down in such a way that his backside was an easy target for the toe of his senior's shoe.

'Leave-out days' were great occasions; there were about seven each year. I spent several at Oak Grove, my Uncle Alfred's house near Eastleigh. We used to play golf at Stoneham and, in the summer, tennis. Sometimes I went to the Powell's at Heroncourt near Farnham. Robin Farmiloe invited me twice to their house on Hampstead Heath and I remember seeing Jack Buchanan and Elsie Randolph in a musical comedy. One memorable day in my last year, Malcolm fetched me in his car and took me to Ewsott where he was a second lieutenant in a light regiment RA which was equipped with 3.7 in. howitzers (the famous screw guns) which were transported on mule-back. Malcolm and I went for a long ride in the morning and in the afternoon I played in a 'fun' game of mule polo. The ball used to remain stationary for long periods. For several minutes I failed to persuade my mount to get close enough to the ball for me to have a swing at it. However, at last I got into a favourable position, swung at the ball and before I could regain control of the mule, found myself back at the stables!

David Wilson was my closest friend in Furley's. His father was then Governor of Bombay, so we had David to stay with us at The Croft sometimes during the holidays. I visited his house at Wokingham once when his father was home on leave. David went to Oxford where he got a Blue for squash and then he was commissioned into the Green Jackets. Sadly, he was killed in the Western desert in 1942.

Robin Farmiloe went into his family business, but volunteered to fight in the Spanish Civil War. When he returned from that, I had a chance meeting with him in London. I suggested that we should lunch together and he answered, 'Great, but would you mind lunching in my restaurant?'

'I didn't know that you had gone into the restaurant business,' I replied, to which his answer was 'Nor did I until this morning, but apparently I bought one last night'!

We found the restaurant in Greek Street. Robin introduced himself to the manager and we had a superb lunch. I did not see Robin again. He joined the Commandos and was killed in the Commando landing in Syria in 1940.

Meanwhile at home, Malcolm bought a two-seater Jowett in 1927. I went up to London with him to collect the car from Waterloo Bridge garage. We had an exciting drive home. Before we had gone three hundred yards one of the front wheels got caught in a tram line, which almost caused a collision. Then later on, Malcolm missed his gear change on Shooters Hill and with a tram clanking its bell just behind us he had great difficulty in starting the car on the steep gradient.

Every term we all used to go up to London and go to a theatre matinee before I caught the school train. We saw all the Aldwych farces—Ralph Lynn, Tom Walls, Winifred Shotter. We also saw the great musical comedy 'Rose Marie'. Leslie Henson was a great favourite of mine.

Life at The Croft continued in its most enjoyable way. We had frequent dinner parties and I took great pleasure in listening to all the reminiscing that went on. My father and mother were both very good, in their own very different ways, at recounting exciting or amusing experiences.

My father gave up his job in 1929 and bought Kingsmere in Shawford. Our garden went down to the river Itchen and one could walk all the way to Winchester along the tow path.

It was not until we settled in Kingsmere that we had our first wireless set. Kingsmere, like The Croft, had no electricity laid on. The lighting and heating was all gas and the water heated by solid fuel burners or by geysers. We always used to go up to bed with candles.

Our Christmas holidays 1929/30 coincided with Malcolm's embarkation leave when he was posted to India. We spent a very happy holiday in a rented house in Weymouth. The whole family enjoyed it very much. Then came the sad day when we all drove to Southampton and saw Malcolm off on his troopship. I had a terrible premonition that I would never see him again.

To my relief I passed the Army Exam well enough to obtain a place in the Woolwich list. If I had missed Woolwich and had had to go to Sandhurst, my Uncle Alfred had promised me that if I went into the King's Own Scottish Borderers, he would pay for my complete set of uniform.

I left Winchester in July 1930, still a rather shy and very naive young man. I had stopped growing when I was just sixteen and looked, as indeed I was, very young for my age.

Mathematics was my best subject and I learnt a lot of physics and a smattering of chemistry. Looking back, most of the knowledge I gained at Winchester, apart from the maths and science, has proved to have been of very little use to me. For example, I can still recite the Latin prepositions which take the ablative case. Carved into my memory is that the future infinitive passive is the supine in -um plus -ire. I had to write that out 2,000 times. I can also recite the roll of Old Wykehamists killed in the South African war. That was because for my first few halves in Chapel, I was in the Lady Chapel and had to turn right before reciting the Creed. This brought me face to face with the South African war Roll of Honour, which I always tried to read through five times during the Creed. This came in handy after the war, when I was sitting at the dinner table at Kingsmere, having a second glass of port and listening to my father and one of his contemporaries talking about a mutual friend of their school days—his name was Hitchens. My father said, 'Wasn't he killed in the South African War?'

His friend said, 'I didn't know that.' So I chimed in: 'Abadie, Barnett, Bright, Brodie, Burton . . . Fisher, Fisher, Grove, Harris, Hitchens—yes, he was!'

I must mention the don who was undoubtedly the greatest personality on the staff—E.R. (Rockley) Wilson. Since 1919 he had regularly played cricket for Yorkshire in August, and just as regularly he had topped the Yorkshire bowling averages, and occasionally the first class English bowling averages. He toured Australia with the MCC team in 1922/23. He was tactless enough to write an article for the Australian press criticising the fairness of the umpires. This made him so unpopular with the spectators that he was provided with a police escort. At one game a spectator dodged the escort and made straight for Rockley, who prepared to defend himself. However, the man asked Rockley if he might shake his hand. Rockley, taken aback, lamely asked him why he wanted to. The man replied, much to Rockley's amusement, 'Well, Mr Wilson, before you came out here, I was the most unpopular man in Australia!' He turned out to be a mass swindler—Australia's equivalent to Hatry or Horatio Bottomley.

One further story about this most popular don. At morning Chapel one day, the Chaplain announced the number of the hymn to be sung, but the organist started to play the music for a different, but equally well known one. Chaos ensued. Some tried to sing the words of the announced hymn to the wrong tune; others tried to remember the words of the hymn which we usually sang to the music which the organ was playing. Winchester College was being made to look very stupid. Suddenly a well-known voice from behind the choir called out, 'NO BALL!' Stunned silence was followed by laughter. The Chaplain gave out the correct hymn number. Rockley Wilson had saved the side again.

3

RMA Woolwich

I had been warned by many people that I would find the first three or four weeks of my first term sheer hell. But, strangely, I did not. It was hectic in the extreme. We had two or sometimes three sessions each day being instructed in Infantry drill under Drill Sergeant McGarrity of the Irish Guards. He was a fine man. He swore at us often but always finished up with the words 'Sir' or 'Gentlemen'. Soon after we left The Shop, he won a top prize in the Irish sweep, retired from the Army, and bought a pub in Windsor.

We also had a lot of PT and a great deal of practical work in digging and revetting trenches, putting up barbed wire fences and so on, all interspersed with lectures. Normally there was a ten minute interval between sessions, but if a change of kit was required we were allowed fifteen minutes. It was a mad rush. For example, if a PT period followed an ID parade, we had to dash back to our rooms, roll up our puttees, take off boots, breeches, and everything else, put on gym vest, white socks and PT shoes and get up to the gymnasium. Then probably you would be awarded a hoxter if one of your socks was not correctly turned down. Hoxter parades took place at reveille and were either drill parades done at the double or fatigues, mostly digging, or filling in what had been dug the previous day! But in spite of all this, the extra freedom that one was given I appreciated greatly, being able to go to the town without having to get permission, or to go to the cinema or to Lewisham Hippodrome when one wanted to. It was bliss. We only had one riding parade each week, so we did not progress very far. I was worried after one ride because I could not get my horse, Lawyer, to canter correctly, although I knew that I was applying the right aids. I told a friendly senior about this. He said, 'Oh, old Lawyer, the only way to make him canter with the right foot leading is to hum "The Bonnets of Bonnie Dundee".' It worked too. I never had any more trouble with Lawyer.

I played in the first soccer eleven for the first half dozen matches, including one against the Old Wykehamists, whose team included Alan Young who had been our senior prefect of Furley's in my last year, and about four other members of the school eleven. Unfortunately I was made to play at outside left, and I had never been able to kick very well with my left foot. The laced leather footballs, especially when they were wet, were very difficult to kick any distance. Our very first match was against Lloyds Bank on their ground at Fairlop, just north of Ilford. It was the first time in my life that I had ever been further north than London! Before the end of the season, I dropped down into the second eleven, where I was much happier, and our season finished in triumph. The two elevens went over to Sandhurst. Our first eleven won 1—0 and the second eleven, 4—0. General Wagstaffe was delighted and told us to celebrate in London, but to be back by 2 a.m. We did just that.

I rather dreaded the Snooker boxing competition. I met a fairly inoffensive cadet in the first round, who was a bit taller than I. After one round, my second, our APTC instructor, told me to give him a hard blow in the stomach and 'he'll crumple up'. I did that, and to my surprise he crumpled up! The next day I had to fight Prem Singh Gyani, who came into the ring in his pugri. During the first round he ducked under my lead and I dislodged his pugri; his long hair tumbled down his face. The fight was stopped while his hair was restored to the shelter of his pugri. The judges' decision was a narrow win for Gyani, but the loser was praised for the way he had coped with his opponent's considerably longer reach, so I felt that I had salvaged my honour. Gyani, an extremely nice man, became Chief of the General Staff of the Indian Army. So our term produced two Chiefs of General Staff, as George Baker, most deservedly, became CGS and was promoted to Field Marshal.

The second term included much more academic work. The maths was interesting as it involved all the mathematics of survey. It then changed to engineering maths, which I never really grasped. This included Young's modulus of elasticity, and such equally dull things. We had civilian professors to teach maths and science, and we all agreed that they were hopeless teachers. They found it very difficult to keep order, because they could not award the dreaded hoxters. On the other hand, Professor Boswell, who taught us political science and economics, was excellent.

We had much more riding instruction, and went out map reading, map making, and on tactical exercises.

I got into the cricket eleven—I had more nets on the County ground at Southampton during my fortnight's recess in early April. Our first match was against the MCC. To our horror, G.O. (Gubby) Allen, who played for Middlesex, and soon afterwards captained England against Australia, was in the team to get some pre-season bowling practice. I went in at number six when our score was about twenty for four wickets. Allen was, of course, much too good for us and we were all out for 88. I was not out 37. I was immediately promoted to bat at number two from then on.

Our next match was against the Army, and we won the toss. Captain Ben Walford, the Army fast bowler, who also played country cricket, was playing. I asked my senior partner if he was going to take the first over, and he said, 'No, you are.' I saw a huge ginger headed man out on the field, and I correctly guessed that he was Walford. He had the reputation of being very fast but dangerously wild, unlike Gubby Allen, who was exceedingly fast, but very accurate. I took a long time taking guard and looking at the field placing, all the time praying to God to assist me. I took my stance and watched him accelerating on his long run. Suddenly, as he passed the umpire, he tripped somehow and came an awful cropper. Thinking that the Almighty had gone rather too far in answer to my prayers, I ran up to him and said, 'I'm awfully sorry, sir.' He was carried off on a stretcher and took no further part in the match.

We were really a very poor side. Terence O'Brien Butler, I, and Pease, who was Eton's twelfth man the year before, were the only ones to make many runs, and Oram and Legs Lyon were the best of the bowlers. I had to bowl quite a lot, but was not sufficiently penetrative to take many wickets. We were always up against much stronger teams, which was very good experience. Sandhurst beat us fairly easily, but we travelled up to Cranwell (Lincolnshire—quite easily my record northern experience) where we managed to win our two-day match.

Earlier in the term, before the April recess, Captain Ames my Company Commander had difficulty in raising a Milocarian (Combined Service Officers) Club team, to run a cross country steeplechase against Sandhurst. He invited Winwood (a very good long distance runner) and me to make up the team. Just before we were to leave in his car, he had a message that someone else had dropped out, so I suggested that Legs Lyon might be a reasonable replacement. We had a most enjoyable day. The course was mostly along sandy rides and deep heather, and was about 5½ miles. Winwood came third, I was 20th, and Legs 33rd out of 34. The 34th was Sandhurst's cross country captain. Ames gave us supper in London and we went to the theatre before returning to The Shop.

I thoroughly enjoyed our last term when we were seniors. George Baker was our Senior Under-Officer and he was outstandingly good; he was also captain of the rugger fifteen.

I captained the second eleven soccer, and played at centre half. Legs was our goal keeper. We played sides much more skilful than ours, but we were so fit, and our morale was so high, that we won most of our matches, including the one against Sandhurst. The first eleven drew their match.

In the early thirties, the country was going through a severe economic crisis, and so the Army, among all other organisations, had to make drastic cuts in expenditure. One result of this was that for our annual camp in the Aldershot area, instead of going by train, we had to go on bicycles. Going down there the plan was that we should spend one night at Hounslow Barracks, and that the next day we should represent a cavalry advance guard going through hostile country to engage the enemy. So we went off, my company leading in company columns in half sections (i.e., in columns of two) at the correct cavalry spacing: five feet from tail to nose. All went well until we were going down Blackheath Hill, when one of our leaders got his wheel stuck in a tramline and fell off. This caused a most embarrassing pile up of the rest of the Company, and a large number of bicycles became casualties. The exercise from Hounslow to Aldershot was a great success and was much enjoyed. Our return journey to Woolwich was accomplished in one day without mishap; we were allowed extended intervals (ten feet from nose to tail) when going down steep hills.

What I enjoyed more than anything else at Woolwich was riding, and the unbelievable improvement in performance we achieved under the brilliant instruction of our 'rough riders'—the sergeant instructors of the Riding Troop RHA. They were most admirable individuals as well as great horse-masters. The cadets in any one ride covered a very wide range of previous experience, from nil to being experienced in the hunting field. Very soon everyone in the ride could run alongside his horse and at the given command vault onto his horse's back at the trot or canter, like a film cowboy. We spent much of the time riding without stirrups and when we started jumping we had to drop the reins just before the horse took off. Inevitably, every ride included one or two cadets who found it all rather difficult. These prompted our rough rider to show his knowledge of the Bible. 'Mr W-- sir, if Jesus Christ rode his donkey into Jerusalem as you're riding that 'orse, no wonder they crucified him, sir.' One of our less talented riders was named Paul. A series of mistakes made by him reduced the instructor to drop to his knees on the tan, look up to the roof and say, 'Paul, Paul, why persecutest thou me?'—a very slight misquotation from the Acts of the Apostles.

My last term, I had two most enjoyable days out with the RA drag hunt. I got into our Company riding team and we won the competition. I also got into the demonstration team which was formed and trained for Mahatma Gandhi's visit to The Shop. Unfortunately Gandhi's visit was cancelled at the last minute, but our display went on. It was held in the Repository. The climax was when each of us in quick succession went down a lane of about six four-foot fences. As we jumped the last one, we had to hold our saddles above our heads, having unstrapped the girths and wriggled clear of the saddles while going over the previous jumps!

Our Seniors' concert took place a day or two later and I remember that we retained in it a reference to the Mahatma's visit:

'Gandhi came to see The Shop
Clad only in a dhoti
The ladies were all rather shocked
And wished he'd worn a coatee.'

They were great days. I had grown up, had put on a stone in weight, and never before or since have I been fitter.

It may be of interest that during my time at The Shop, to avoid getting hoxters for long hair, I had to have my hair cut at least once a week. Fortunately, the cost was 6d (2½p) as compared with the £2.20 which I have to pay now—fortunately once every two months!

Larkhill

I was commissioned in January 1932, a month before my twentieth birthday. My commission was signed by King George V. My pay was nine shillings and ten pence a day.

I was given a month's leave before joining the Young Officers Course at the School of Artillery at Larkhill. During my leave I bought a second hand Jowett touring car for £30. It had only two cylinders, one on either side of the engine, no self-starter, and a manual windscreen wiper. It was a four-seater, but had only one door, which was on the passenger's side in front. The back of the front seat folded forwards to allow the back seat passengers to take their seats. I was very proud of it. But more anon!

I remember how impressed Dick—then at Copthorne—was, that every day of my leave I was actually earning almost ten shillings a day while enjoying our normal routine of family golf and cinemagoing. The day soon came for me to set out on my first solo run in my car—the 31 miles to Larkhill.

I found the course absorbingly interesting; this was proved by my improved results. I was 42nd at the start of the course, and finished in eleventh place.

We were trained on 18-pounders, horse-drawn. In the frequent 'drill orders' we took over all the more interesting and important jobs, while men from the Depot Battery supplied the rest of the four gun battery man-power. The jobs we did were: Battery Commander and his assistant, Gun Position Officer and his assistants, Battery Leader, NCO i/c Signals and his signallers, Nos. 1 & 3 of each gun detachment, and the lead driver of each six-horse gun team. So there was plenty of riding to be done on the wide expanses of Salisbury Plain. Even so, one of our officers managed somehow to wind his six-horse team round a solitary tree or post. Laying the telephone line from the OP to the gun position was a great experience. It was laid from reels carried by two mounted signallers, normally at a canter in a straight line, and subsequently improved by being raised on posts or buried under crossings of roads or tracks. We also learnt other equipments, and the gun drill of 3.7" howitzers, 4.5" and 6" howitzers, and 60 pounder guns.

We found time for occasional rounds of golf and, when the cricket season opened, to play against local villages and such teams. I played a lot of squash and very much enjoyed my first experience of living in an Officers Mess. In the last week of our course we had a lecture on etiquette from a subaltern's point of view, and general hints on how to become an efficient section commander. This was most brilliantly given by a senior subaltern on leave from India—Ambrose Pratt—of whom more later. Legs Lyon and I plucked up courage and asked Pratt whether it would be in order for us to apply to play in a Regimental Gunner match before joining our first Brigades. He was all for it, and told us to whom to apply, and said he would prepare the ground for us with the match manager.

After our final Guest Night, friction between two rival cliques boiled up. Our clique kidnapped the leader of the other clique and removed his trousers; somehow I found myself driving my Jowett across Salisbury Plain with the struggling hostage and six escorts in it. We dumped him some four miles away. Next morning I found that in revenge the opposition clique had put half a pound of sugar in my petrol tank, which did it no good at all. A friendly artificer very kindly drained my tank and flushed out the petrol system, and I was able to get to Kingsmere on time!

Legs and I duly played for the Gunners against the I Zingari, a two day match. We had a very strong batting side. I was put down to go in sixth. Our opening pair, Hudson and Hamilton, normally expected to provide an opening stand of over 50, but were both out cheaply, and our fourth wicket fell at 84. Our captain, Colonel Rawson, as I went out to bat said to me, 'Now's the time to make a name for yourself.' Everything went right for me and I was eventually last out, having scored 87 out of our total of 210. Before close of play, Legs had taken the only two wickets to have fallen. I sent a telegram to Kingsmere giving them the good news. The opposition included G.F. Earle, the then captain of Somerset, Lewis Weighall who had selected me to play for the Prep. Schools at Lords seven years previously, and the Army fast bowler whose name I have forgotten. The guest night that evening was an unforgettable experience. The civilians wore tails and white ties. I was amazed at how elderly people could behave after dinner, so boisterously. 'Cockfighting' and 'Are you there, Moriarty' were both played. One of the guests found great fun in holding the tails of an evening coat in his two hands and jerking them apart, so that the tail coat split right up to the collar. There followed billiard fives, and tobogganing down a flight of stone steps, treated with soapy water, on tea trays. One had to time one's roll off the tray accurately, as there was a wall about fifteen feet from the bottom of the staircase.

The second day of the match was fairly routine. We declared our second innings with two wickets down, and won the match. Three days later I got a cable from Malcolm saying, 'Congratulations on your regimental debut. Now get into the side for Lords.' In those days, letters to India took three weeks; somebody must have sent a cable to Malcolm. I know it was not my parents, and I suspect that it was Ambrose Pratt, though he never admitted it. My morale was sky high.

Our postings came through from the War Office just before we left Larkhill. To my delight both Lionel Lewin and I were posted to 21st Field Brigade at Catterick.

During my time at Larkhill, I had my first flight in an aeroplane, and my one and only ascent in a captive ballon.

Catterick 1932—1934

Lionel Lewin and I arranged to meet at Bawtry on the Great North Road so that we could do the final eighty-odd miles in convoy. His snub-nosed Morris Cowley and my Jowett both behaved perfectly and we arrived at the Officers Mess, Somme Lines, at tea time. The Mess was a single storey building which had obviously started life as a wooden hut and had later been bricked up. It had one very windblown tree in front of it, and other bricked up huts on either side which were the single officers' quarters. Lionel and I had to share a quarter, which consisted of a small living room with fire place, an armchair, a table and a hard chair; and a bedroom with an iron bedstead, a chair, a chest of drawers, and a cupboard. Lionel, being senior to me, chose the room with the fireplace, for which in the winter we got a scuttleful of coal per day. Before long we changed our organisation and got both beds into the bedroom and both armchairs into the living room. In the two and a half years we stayed there, even after the number of occupants was increased by two dogs, we very rarely had a cross word or a growl.

My Battery Commander was Major J.G.M.B. Cooke, a small, fat, very inarticulate bachelor. I was in P Field Battery, and Lionel was in Q Battery, commanded by Lieutenant Colonel E.W.G. Wilson, who was married. One of the other Battery Commanders was a single man, and the fourth was Keith Dunn, who, in my humble opinion, was the best Battery Commander I ever knew. He was an ex-adjutant of The Shop, and an ex-Chief Instructor at Weedon, the Army Equitation School. My Battery Captain was Bob Aitken, who left soon after my arrival; he went on an attachment to the Canadian RHA. Before he left, he declared that he was jolly well going to find an American Heiress to marry. We were not unduly surprised to receive a cable from him a month or two later, saying, 'engaged to Miss Ingersoll'! My fellow subalterns were Ted Howard Vyse and 'Sailor' Kitcat. I was extremely lucky to have Ted as my senior subaltern. He was a most efficient officer, completely unselfish and most helpful. I learnt all my duties from him, including those of Brigade orderly officer. After I had been there a fortnight, I was appointed orderly officer for the first time, fully confident that I knew exactly what to do under any circumstances, thanks to Ted's instruction. I got up at reveille and was almost dressed, when there was a knock at the door. It was the Brigade orderly sergeant.

'I believe that you are orderly officer, sir.' Feeling very important, I confirmed the fact. 'Would you come to Z Battery stables, sir. I think Gunner H—— has hung himself.'

I went numb; why had Ted not told me what to do now? I went down, and by the time I arrived Gunner H—— had been cut down. I made certain that the Medical Officer had been sent for, and retired to a loose box, where a surprised charger saw me being violently sick on his bedding. I then told the Adjutant and the Battery Commander what had happened, and returned to the stables until I was relieved by a Z Battery officer. What a start! I had no breakfast that day.

I was flattered that news of my success for the Regiment against I Zingari had reached the 21st Field Brigade before my arrival. The Brigade had already reached the final of the Garrison Cricket Cup, and so I was just in time to play in the final against the Durham Light Infantry. We won the final. I was selected to play for Catterick Garrison's last match of the season, and managed to score my first century since leaving Sandrock Hall.

The great attraction of being stationed at Catterick was the wonderful opportunity it gave one for first class hunting with famous hunts—the Zetland and the Bedale. Our brigade had been mechanised the year before I joined it, but had been allowed to keep fifteen troop horses, officially for teaching NCOs to ride. Naturally, the horses retained were all good hunters. Junior officers could hire one of these for 15 shillings per month for the whole hunting season. Every officer was also alloted a charger, and was allowed to provide his own second charger; and thus could have three hunters fed by the Army and looked after by unit grooms and farriers.

I never bought myself a second charger. I wish I had. I could have got a very good light-weight hunter capable of doing well in point to points for about £40. I had 'The Dun' as my charger and 'Victoria' as my 'fifteen bobber'. Dunny was a good-looking horse, but was old and lethargic. Victoria was ugly, with coarse, uncomfortable paces, but was a very keen jumper, rather inclined to rush her jumps. Between them, they served me well for my first hunting season, throughout which I averaged three days hunting per fortnight. There were no horse boxes, so we used to hack out to all the meets, some of which involved us with a sixteen- or on one occasion a twenty-mile hack. I greatly enjoyed it. One day soon after the hunting season started, the Bedale had a meet very close to Somme Lines, but I was Brigade orderly officer. During the morning I met our CO, Colonel Longmore, in Barracks; he was a very sick man and shortly afterwards was invalided out of the Army. He had been a very keen horseman. He called me over to him and said, 'Haigy, aren't the Bedale meeting at Scorton today? Why aren't you out with them?' I told him that I was orderly officer, and had been unable to find anyone to stand in for me. At this, to my surprise, he called me a bloody fool and told me I should have asked him to carry out my duties, which he would have been glad to do!

When the brigade was mechanised, it was given all the vehicles of the very first field brigade to have been mechanised and which had been re-equipped with more modern vehicles. Our gun towers were Burford Kegresses, which had wheels in front and rubber tracks instead of the rear wheels. They had proved reasonably satisfactory at Bulford on Salisbury Plain, but on the soft gradients of the moors and dales, and in particular on boggy ground, they were useless. Our technical vehicles were Crossley Kegresses, also half tracked, and were equally hopeless on our moorland training area. I found this particularly frustrating. Our training was excellent, our guns and vehicles looked superb, and yet on the local roads a battery had the appearance of being a shambles, as it was impossible to keep the correct vehicle distances as the vehicles had such poor performance.

It may be of interest to any young reader if I describe the lot of Other Ranks. Every one of them was a volunteer, and a large number of them, mostly miners, had recently been unemployed. All were on at least six year engagements and most of the NCOs had signed on from 12 to 21 years.

Each barrack room was one hut, which also contained a senior NCO's 'loose box' and a washroom. The barrack room slept up to 24 men. Each man had an iron bed with three biscuits, which formed one mattress. The beds, when not in use, telescoped up to form a seat, using a biscuit as a seat and two as a backrest. They also each had a steel cupboard attached to the wall above their beds. The room was heated by a single sawyer stove in the centre of the room and was lit by two pendant electric lights. The communal furniture consisted of two trestle tables and four benches, all very basic. They had an excellent NAAFI which provided billiards, darts, and so on, as well as a wet and a dry canteen, and, fairly frequently, films or concert parties. I forget now what the basic rates of pay were then, but at the weekly pay parade very few gunners drew more than fifteen shillings (75p). In the camp were two cinemas and a Sands Home.

They always seemed very contented and were a most cheerful and likeable lot. Both my Number Ones (sub-section commanders) had had war service; one of them, Sergeant Harding, had won a Military Medal during the war. His barrack room always won the Challenge Shield awarded annually for the best-kept barrack room at weekly inspections. At one weekly inspection I did my usual inspection prior to that of the Battery Commander, and I spotted that one pair of boots on top of a locker had the spurs on the wrong boots. I pointed this out to Sergeant Harding. When I accompanied Major Cooke on his inspection a few minutes later, the gunner with the offending spurs was standing to attention beside his bed. I noticed that he had a badly bruised cheek and eye. I made no comment, but Sergeant Harding later volunteered that he had sent for the gunner and 'the poor kid', in reaching up to put the correct spurs on to the correct boots had unluckily caught his eye on the door of his locker. Discipline was obviously brutal at times.

The Officers Mess was very comfortable. It had a billiard room, a squash court and a hard tennis court. Our messing cost us 2/6 (12½p) per day; half a pint of beer cost 3½d and a glass of sherry 7d. My average monthly mess bill was normally under £7, which included hunt subscriptions. To illustrate how well off we were on our 9/10 per day: Lionel had no private means at all, as his mother was a war widow and very badly off. He had been educated free at Wellington. He ran a car, hunted three days a fortnight, travelled frequently to play rugger for the Gunners at Woolwich, and went to Darlington every Saturday evening with me, for a mixed grill and a visit to the cinema. After eighteen months, he had saved enough money to send his mother a cheque for £100!

Every other summer we went to practice camp at Redesdale, on the Scottish Borders, for live firing. On my first day on the ranges, I was as usual Left Section Commander, and had to kneel behind my two guns and make certain that they were properly laid, and so on. My first job was to go to the command post to identify the battery aiming point. I looked through the director and saw that the aiming point was the left-hand edge of a far distant copse. I rushed to my two guns to indicate the aiming point; Sergeant Harding shouted to his layer, 'Aiming point same as two years ago'! With such continuity, no wonder that it was such an efficient unit!

Each officer conducted at least one shoot from the OP. Mine was successful. At the end of one day, as I was acting as Battery Leader, some dummy tanks appeared (where Cooke had told me they would) and I had to wheel the column off the road just below a convenient crest and engage them with observed fire. The first two guns went a little too far down the slope and were unable to engage the tanks as the shells would not have cleared the crest. I engaged the target with the other two guns reasonably successfully. At the post mortem on the day's shooting, the CRA asked me why two of my guns had not been able to fire at the tanks. I told him that they had gone further down the slope so that they could engage the tanks through open sights if they came over the ridge. This satisfied him, though I do not think that he believed me!

In October 1932 we heard that Malcolm, who was then in a mountain battery at Wana, had been put on the Seriously Ill list. He had been hit on the head by a hockey ball and subsequently on two occasions had overslept to such a degree that nobody could wake him up for hours. He was eventually embarked on a troopship to have his trouble diagnosed at Mill Bank. I went on leave just before Christmas for a period to include Malcolm's arrival at Southampton. On Boxing Day evening my father and mother, Aunt Evelyn, Dick and I were in the drawing room playing some of Malcolm's gramophone records, when the telephone rang in the hall. I answered it. It was the Shawford postmistress.

'Mr Tony, there is a telegram for your father, will you take it? It's bad news, I'm afraid.' It was from the War Office, saying that Malcolm had died of heart failure on Christmas night and had been buried at sea. I sat in the dark for a minute or two, then opened the drawing room door and asked Dad to come out. I broke the news to him and we returned to the drawing room to tell the others. I am ashamed to say that I was useless at consoling my parents and, in fact, my poor mother had to come upstairs to comfort me. It was a terrible shock. Malcolm had longed to get into a Mountain Battery. He had seen action in the North West Frontier area, had won the local point to point and was a whipper-in for the Wana Hunt.

I celebrated my twenty-first birthday two months later. Lionel and I drove in to Darlington in the afternoon. I bought my birthday present from my parents—a portable HMV wireless set. We then had our usual mixed grill and went and saw a film. It was snowing hard as we started home. When we got to our riding school my 'Jow' got stuck in a snow drift. We emptied the radiator and lit a safety lamp and put it under the bonnet. We then struggled through deep snow, taking it in turns to carry the 'portable' set. It had a strap handle on top, which was useless for us as the bottom of the set would have been in the snow! As well as the set, we had to carry the large high tension battery and two accumulators which came with it. We 'made it' eventually, and the wireless brightened up our quarter and gave me great pleasure wherever I went until I finally went to Egypt five years later.

The next summer we took part in manoeuvres which were held locally. I was appointed as an umpire. My main task in the defensive battle was to obtain the Brigade's fire plan, then to gallop off on Victoria to the targets as they were engaged, and tell the recipients what casualties they had sustained. I thoroughly enjoyed myself. I had a trumpeter as my horse holder. He impressed me greatly by his ability to drink a bottle of ginger beer out of the bottle at the trot! For one fortnight, Ted and I were sent to help a TA Field Brigade with their practice camp at Redesdale. They were a most amusing outfit and entertained us lavishly.

During the summer I played cricket for the Gunners at Woolwich, Aldershot and Portsmouth. The Garrison match which I enjoyed most was against Rossall School. We stayed the night in Blackpool and had a rare old time. I was also invited to play for Sir William Worsley's eleven against the Free Foresters. Sir William was then captain of Yorkshire and was the present Duchess of Kent's father. I stayed the two nights at Hovingham Hall and much appreciated the feudal atmosphere which pervaded the Hall and the whole village.

Earlier in the year I had heard that General Eden's golden retriever bitch was going to have puppies. We knew the Edens very well as they lived in Shawford, quite close to Kingsmere. I asked if they would let me buy one. In due course I heard that they were going to put the puppy in the guard's van of a train at Shawford station, and that the very same guard's van would arrive at Darlington station some ten hours later. I took my batman, Gunner Riley, who happened to have worked in kennels, to meet the train in Darlington. I bought a dog's campbed for Whisky and we returned to Somme Lines in triumph. A few weeks previously Lionel had inherited 'Bobby', who had the head of a very good-looking fox terrier but who had a chassis more like a dachshund. They became great friends and, thanks largely to Gunner Riley, Whisky developed into a very beautiful healthy dog. Unfortunately, on his first visit to Kingsmere he misbehaved himself and my mother said that I must leave him behind in Catterick when next I went down. She relented however, and the day before I was to go there again a telegram arrived saying curtly, 'Bring your dog'. When we arrived my mother apologised for the wording of the telegram, 'but what would Mrs W. at the post office have thought if I had said "Bring whisky"!'

That short leave was in connection with the Gunner match against the Navy at Portsmouth. It was a two day match, and after it I would have two days at home before returning to Catterick for the CRA's inspection. During the second day of the match, I got a telegram from the Adjutant saying, 'CRA's inspection brought forward two days. Essential you be on parade 0830 tomorrow.' We were in grave danger of defeat and the Navy claimed the extra half hour to try to get us out. I was batting and with my partner we remained not out when stumps were drawn at 7.30, allowing me under thirteen hours to be on parade three hundred miles away. I sped back to Kingsmere, collected my night things and Whisky and, after a quick snack, left just before 10 p.m. By this time Jow had developed two faults which made driving more tiring. It used to fall out of top gear unless you held the gear lever, and its one and only door used to fly open. So I had to tie string to the door handle and sit on the end of the string. I have never enjoyed a journey less. After getting on to the Great North Road, I twice dozed off and was woken up by hitting the kerb. We made it with three quarters of an hour to spare. Whisky had slept soundly on the back seat all the way, despite my vocal efforts trying to stop myself going to sleep.

Travel by car was absurdly cheap. Petrol cost under sixpence a gallon.

During the summer I passed the Dun on to a newly joined subaltern and amid great excitement two chargers arrived for Lionel and me. Mine was a three-quarter bred chestnut, and Lionel's a good looking grey. I called mine Firebrand as he was sired by Mars, a well-known Irish stallion. His paces were beautifully smooth; his manners left something to be desired as he was a bad-tempered kicker and after jumping he used to buck quite unnecessarily. Both Keith Dunn and Ted Howard Vyse helped me to try to cure him of these faults, but we were not completely successful. So Firebrand had to wear a red riband on his tail when out hunting, and one could never relax too much in case he started his bucking.

We won the Garrison cricket again and, as a reward 'Brother' Walsh our Adjutant and I took the eleven to Scarborough to watch the Australians play. The Jow had great difficulty in getting up Sutton Bank and I had to make my passengers dismount and walk the final bit of the hill. We had a most enjoyable day but I must admit that my passengers, well as they behaved, made me realise how immature and naive I was!

We had a Mess invitation for two officers to attend the Bishop of Durham's At Home at Barnard Castle. The Mess Secretary and I were detailed to represent the Brigade. We went dressed for tennis (in the bottom corner of the invitation the word 'tennis' appeared in brackets). As we turned into the Palace gates all we could see was masses of top hatted men in frock coats and ladies in Ascot dresses. Richards told me to get out of the car and ask a gardener whether in fact there were tennis courts prepared for the day. He assured me that there were. So we parked our slightly scruffy Riley among all the Diamlers and Bentleys and went in search. We found a little curate with a racquet and a bag of balls. He took us to the superb courts and eventually two other men arrived to play. The curate beat a hasty retreat, whereupon we had four excellent sets. We suddenly became aware of a tall figure standing watching us. To our horror we realised it was the Bishop himself. He said, 'I just came to make certain that you have had some tea.' I looked towards the car park; our car was almost the only one still there. Bishop Hemsley Henson was horrified that no-one on his staff had got us in for tea. He insisted that Richards and I should stay to supper. We did so. He was a wonderful host and regaled us with most amusing stories and a glass or two of excellent wine. During supper the Bishop told me that he was a cousin of Leslie Henson, my long-time favourite comedian. Before we left he had invited us to join his party for the Durham County Ball.

Ted Howard Vyse was posted to the Riding Troop RHA and we received Frank Weldon straight from his YO's course. Latterly Ted had been doing a lot of schooling of steeplechasers to help our local trainer, Lyde. This involved driving over to Richmond early most mornings. When Ted left, Mr Lyde asked me if I would be prepared to help him out occasionally with schooling over jumps. I was delighted; apart from anything else I had never ridden a thoroughbred before. I did it for about four weeks until he increased his staff. It was great experience, but it became rather too much like hard work to do that three days a week before breakfast. However Mr Lyde rewarded me by giving me two rides in a National Hunt meeting at Catterick Bridge. One was in an amateur riders' steeplechase over two miles, in which I finished fifth in a field of twelve. The other was a two-mile hurdle race in which I was the only amateur taking part, and predictably finished last of nine runners.

This would be an appropriate time to mention that Ted Howard Vyse represented Great Britain in the Berlin Olympic Games in 1937 at cross country riding. Sailor Kitcat won the Prince of Wales Cup at Earls Court for Combined Services show jumping. Frank Weldon captained the Olympic gold medal winning team for three day eventing after the Second World War, and won the individual gold medal himself. Such were the only other subalterns in P Battery at the same time as me!

Each year we had a Gunner point to point race of the old-fashioned type. We were taken to the start and pointed out a tent pitched in the distance. We had to go round that and finish over the last fence of the Zetland point to point course. You chose your own course and were guaranteed no barbed wire if you kept within a quarter of a mile of the direct lines from start to tent and tent to finish. I rode Victoria in my first season and finished after most of the other competitors; in my second season I was, I think, close to the lead on Firebrand, when he slipped and went lame.

For my last year at Catterick, P Battery was down to three officers. Miles Brittain was commanding, I was acting Battery Captain and Gun Position Officer, and Frank Weldon was Battery Leader. We had Practice Camp at Redesdale and manoeuvres in South Yorkshire. It was a most rewarding time.

In November 1934 my posting to the 2nd AA Brigade at Portsmouth came through. I was disappointed because I had hoped to go to RHA, for which I had been recommended, but apparently Colonel Gillett, who was a friend of my father's and who was on the Gunner cricket selection committee, had asked for me to go to Portsmouth and have the chance of playing myself into the Representative Gunner eleven.

My last day's hunting was the best I ever had. There was a meet on the south bank of the Tees. Lionel and I hacked out to it, eighteen miles. Hounds found straight away and we set off over one of the best bits of hunting country of the Zetland. Two hours later the hunt ended in a 'kill'. The local paper described it as a twelve mile point and 21 miles as hounds ran. We then walked the horses back to Somme Lines, a walk of less then six miles!

Eventually, with great regret, I left Catterick early in December. I had a week's leave at Kingsmere, during which I sold the Jowett and replaced it with a small Morris saloon with a sunshine roof and a self starter.

6

Portsmouth and Malta 1934—1936

I reported to 2nd AA Brigade at Clarence Barracks, Southsea, a week before Christmas. It was all very different from Somme Lines. Clarence Barracks housed a medium brigade RA (less one Battery, eight miles away at Fort Fareham), a battalion of the South Staffordshire Regiment, and ourselves. We shared a Mess with the Medium Regiment, a very comfortable three storey brick building which contained all the single officers' quarters. Our offices, stores and vehicle parks were within the barracks, but our guns and instruments were kept at Southsea Castle, about seven minutes walk away across Southsea Common. Our officers were not entitled to chargers nor to grooms nor forage, but the Medium Regiment were, and their chargers were kept at Fort Fareham and were very underused. The whole atmosphere of the place depressed me. My two fellow subalterns in my Battery (4th HAA Battery) were Ted Croft and Ralph Hyatt; the latter I had known in Catterick as he was with the other Field Brigade there. The other ranks seemed not to enjoy life half as much as those in 21st Field, although their living conditions and facilities outside barracks were very much better.

One of my first duties was to help organize and to host the Mess children's Christmas party. During a short rest from my labours, the wife of one of the Medium Regiment's Battery Commanders came up to me and engaged me in polite conversation. I was staggered when she asked me, 'When do you have to go back to school?'! I pointedly fingered my Gunner tie, and she retired in confusion.

Ralph told me that he had managed to borrow one of the Medium Brigade's officers' chargers for the hunting season with the Hambledon hunt. So I went over to Fort Fareham and saw Captain Stuart, who seemed to be the one and only officer who made use of the dozen or so horses. I was very impressed with a bay gelding called 'Second String'. I asked whose charger it was. It belonged to Major Murphy who was in the Medium Brigade. I asked the groom if Major Murphy ever rode the horse and the groom told me that he had never even been up to see the horse and that he himself was the only person who ever rode it. He also told me that Second String was an awful puller and was difficult to control. I returned to the Mess and asked Major Murphy if he would allow me to take his charger out hunting with the Hambledon. He looked at me as if I was mad, but agreed, provided that it was properly insured and that he could not be held responsible financially for anything. I returned to Stuart with my saddle and a double bridle and took Second String out for a hack, and jumped a few obstacles in the paddock. I was delighted with him.

Stuart was very pleased and said that he would ensure that if I gave him 48 hours warning of any meet which I wanted to attend, he would have the groom and the horse at the meet for me at the correct time. I had about six days hunting in the next two months. Second String proved to be a wonderful jumper and perfectly controllable in a double bridle. My day was made when hounds found when the Master and the whole of the hunt were in a narrow lane with no possible exit into open country. The Master was heard to shout, 'Is that new Gunner there?' and I was thrust forward. 'Give me a lead over this wired five bar gate' he ordered. I must say I did not like the look of it, but we cleared ten yards of the lane, cantered collectedly and as near as possible to the left hand hedge, and with the Master close behind me I swung Second String to the right, and the great horse cleared the gate beautifully. The Master's horse refused. I took a good look all round the field and found it to be surrounded by barbed wire. The only thing was to jump back over the gate again, which was not awfully easy. Ralph, seeing my predicament, had kindly waited for me. By arrangement he trotted past the gate while I put Second String to it at as acute an angle as I dared. Again he achieved it. When we caught up with the field, the Master came up specially to ask Ralph and me to dine at his house the next day. I had come good!

I must continue the saga of Second String. There was to be a Combined Services race at the Hursley point to point in April. Stuart, Hyatt and I entered for it, so Ralph and I started training sessions to get our horses fit. The only suitable field was beside the road that went along the crest of the Portsdown Hills. I was riding Second String in a snaffle. We decided to do eight circuits of the field at a 'hunting gallop'. I tried to slow down on the twelfth lap but nothing I did seemed to have any effect on Second String. After about thirty laps, with Ralph laughing his head off, the horse was in a muck sweat and my reins were slippery with sweat, but I thought I could stop him by aiming him at a haystack near the edge of the field. This I did but at the last moment he swerved towards the road and we came face to face with a barbed wire fence and beyond it a bank dropping down to the tarmac road. Thank God Second String saw it through his sweat, jumped it, and landed on the tarmac. I had lost a stirrup and had let go of the reins. By the time I had regained the reins, Second String had crossed the road and set off down a narrower tarmac road down the hill. It was an utter nightmare. There were high banks on either side. One or two startled pedestrians tried to stop us. Eventually we were faced by the main Fareham-Portsmouth road, where an RAC scout was on point duty. He signalled us to stop; I shouted that we were out of control and he managed to stop the traffic on the main road while we rushed on towards Porchester castle. But soon Second String decided that he had had enough, and within two hundred yards of Portsmouth harbour, he pulled up. It was quite the most frightening half hour of my life. We met Ralph walking down the hill. We returned to stables and to my surprise neither then nor the next day did Second String suffer any ill effects from his crazy gallop.

We duly took part in the point to point. My parents came to watch, but I rode him in a pelham bit, which he did not enjoy, and we finished fifth. After the race, however, a member of the Hambledon hunt offered me a ride on his horse in the Members Lightweight race at the Hambledon point to point. That race, despite my inexperience, we won. The horse had also won the same race the year before.

On the whole, I found the work very dull at Clarence Barracks and at Southsea Castle. We were equipped with 3 inch 20 cwt. mobile AA guns, towed by Scamell six-wheelers. The fire control instruments were Predictors and Height Finders. Portsmouth of course had much to offer. The Combined Services sports complex had the County cricket ground and superb football and hockey fields. The Barracks were within five minutes walk of the main shops of Southsea and the various cinemas and the theatre. I played quite a lot of hockey for the Combined Services. I had played a few games at the RMA Woolwich and in fact, to my surprise, was chosen for the Company team at outside right, in preference to a cadet who had played in that position for Clifton's first eleven. But the Combined Services hockey was of far superior quality.

Whisky too did not enjoy life at Portsmouth nearly as much as he had enjoyed Catterick. He missed our rides before breakfast, and going out with the grooms exercising the horses. Here his exercise was confined to two walks to Southsea Castle per day, and the occasional trip out to Fort Fareham to visit Second String. This reminds me of an amusing incident. I had had a day's hunt with the Hambledon and I had handed Second String over to a groom to hack back to Fareham. After divesting myself of my hunting coat and top hat, I got into my little Morris to drive back to Southsea. Going through Portsmouth I thought that various pedestrians were being particularly friendly, waving to me, smiling, and laughing. On arrival at Clarence Barracks, I found the explanation. I had left my top hat on the sunshine roof immediately above my head. It must have looked too stupid!

Soon Ted Croft and I were sent on a three week 'Change of Category' course at the AA school at Biggin Hill. After we had been on the course for a day or two, our Battery Commander designate, Lieutenant Colonel Freddy Morgan, arrived to 'sit in' on our course. By the second week Ted and I thought that Freddy was asking a great many very intelligent questions and so, when he told us that he was going to sit the end of course examination, we worked very studiously and revised every evening, in the hopes that Freddy would not get better marks than us in the exam. The result was, that when the marks came out, Ted and I were awarded 'distinguished' certificates and became equal top, and Freddy's marks were not divulged. We very soon realised how lucky we were to have Freddy as our next Battery Commander. He was a delightful man in every way. Eventually he became General Sir Frederick Morgan, having commanded the Support Group of the 1st Armoured Division in Normandy, and then having been in charge of all the planning of Operation Overlord, the Allied invasion of Normandy. After he left the Army, he was appointed Director of Nuclear Development at Harwell.

As soon as he took over the Battery, everything came to life and morale soared. We went to Watchet on the Somerset coast for our Practice Camp, which seemed to go quite well, and from there we went direct to camp on Salisbury Plain to take part in manoeuvres. We were part of the defending force and we were used in an anti-tank role. At one evening conference, our CO, Colonel Barstow, announced that he wanted to send out an 'officers patrol' on motor bikes next morning, to contact the attacking force and to study and report on their line of advance. I volunteered for the job and was accepted. Only then did I realise that I had never ridden a motor bike! So I got one of our most experienced DRs to give me a crash course that night. Next morning I and three other rank DRs, wearing white hat bands to show we were of the defending force, rode out beyond our front line defences and established ourselves on a hill which, in order to attack our defences, the attacking armour would have to pass either to north or to south. When we saw them, they appeared to be taking the northern route, so I despatched two DRs with a message to our CO. A few minutes later the enemy changed course, heading for the southern route, so I sent my last DR off with another message. I thought that I would stay until the very last moment before racing back. Eventually I seized my bike and completely failed to start it. I then cheated—I took off my white hat band, stopped an enemy vehicle and got one of the crew to start my bike for me. Then I dashed back to Colonel Barstow, remembering to put my white hat band back on. I never confessed that I had had to enlist the enemy's help in getting back safely.

After the battle, we went for a fortnight's camp in Surrey. I was ordered to be in charge of the rail party. I told my batman, Gunner Bridle, to drive my car, with Whisky as passenger, direct to the camp near Brookwood on the afternoon before I left with the rail party. When I arrived at the camp, I was met by a tearful Bridle who told me that he had disobeyed me and had driven from Larkhill to Portsmouth, had shut Whisky in my quarter and then gone on to North End, Portsmouth to spend the night with his wife. When he went to fetch Whisky the next morning, he found the door of my quarter open and Whisky had disappeared. He searched the Barracks and Southsea Castle and then reported the incident to the police. Of course I was furious with him and sent him off the next day to have a thorough search for Whisky, to tell the Medium Brigade and the South Staffordshire Regiment and to revisit the police. He did all this without any success. The next day he got a letter from his wife saying that the previous evening she had been disturbed by a dog continually barking outside her front door. She had opened the door and found Whisky there. He had only been to that house twice previously, and each time he had made the journey, some four miles, by tram with Gunner Bridle. How on earth did he find his way there? Did he go by tram? He never told me!

In between these many training commitments I fitted in some very good cricket matches, mostly for the Gunners and the Combined Services. Then in September I was granted three weeks leave. I spent the first week very pleasantly in Kingsmere and with our usual routine of golf, tennis and cinema-going. Then Whisky and I departed for Catterick. My purpose was to find out whether in March the next year (1935) I could arrange to take Second String up there for a few days hunting and possibly ride him in the open race of one of the Hunt's point to points. I wanted to see if Mr Lyde could help over transport for at least part of the journey, and also whether he or my old Brigade would be prepared to put me up. So off we went. We spent a night in Scarborough and the next day, soon after rejoining the Great North Road, I was stopped by two motor cycle policemen. I wondered frantically what I had done wrong.

'Are you Lieutenant A.E.G. Haig of 2nd Anti Aircraft Brigade, Portsmouth?' I admitted that I was, quaking with fear. 'You are to return to your Brigade as soon as possible.' They did not know why. So I turned round and started the long journey home. I reached Kingsmere at tea time and rang up Freddy Morgan. He told me to spend the night at home and to go and see him next morning. It transpired that our Regiment, reinforced by a Battery from another Brigade, had been ordered at five days notice to go to Malta. Mussolini had invaded Abyssinia, the Mediterranean Fleet had gone to Alexandria, and we were wanted for the Air Defence of Malta.

We had a most hectic five days embarking our guns and vehicles on the SS *Belerephon*, and receiving reinforcements. Our four 4-gun Batteries were made into two eight-gun Batteries and we received another eight-gun Battery from Blackdown, and a Light AA Battery. At our final guest night, during a very rough game of billiard fives, a hard-hit billiard ball ricocheted off my hand onto my mouth. It snapped off one of my front teeth level with the gum, leaving the nerve sticking out of the root, and also damaged the next tooth. This entailed five visits to the dentist in three days!

I deposited Whisky at Kingsmere and we entrained at Portsmouth. We embarked at Southampton in SS *Nevasa*, dressed in service dress, breeches, field boots and spurs, to take on any Italian air forces.

The voyage to Malta took eight days. We struck a storm in the Bay of Biscay but then we had six hours shore leave in Gibraltar, and very pleasant it was too. It seems extraordinary now, but at the age of 22, that was the first time I had set foot outside England, not counting a half-day visit to Edinburgh when I was at Redesdale!

I thoroughly enjoyed the voyage out. Our Regiment had more or less the whole ship to ourselves. The first class accommodation was excellent and the menus had to be seen to be believed. I always thought that our family were big breakfast eaters, but breakfasts on board made our breakfasts at The Croft and at Kingsmere seem almost meals for slimmers!

I was horrified by my first inspection tour of the troop-decks. They were well below the waterline, and of course, air-conditioning had not been thought of. The troops slept in hammocks slung from hooks in the ceiling. The atmosphere was terrible, and the whole place smelt of sweaty socks and sick. Fortunately the weather was good and they were able to spend most of the daylight hours on deck, doing PT, receiving instruction, taking part in boxing tournaments or playing housey-housey (bingo).

The Grand Harbour looked beautiful as we entered it. We disembarked early one morning and marched to Imtarfa Barracks, in the centre of the island, a march of about six miles in huge humidity and with the thermometer reading over 80°F in the shade. We had been issued with khaki drill and topees on board, but arrived at our new home soaked in sweat.

The *Bellerephon* arrived in harbour two days after us, so we had time to settle in before collecting our guns, vehicles and other equipment. By then all our Section positions had been selected for the optimum defence of Valetta and the harbours. My Section position was close to Imquaba, and adjacent to one of the many sandstone quarries. Within a few days we had deployed our guns and instruments, and had built gun pits and instrument pits. This was a tremendous task as the trunions of our guns were at least seven feet from the ground, so the gun pit walls had to be at least eight feet high. Filling the sand bags was not a pleasant task, as Malta had no natural soil and so the filling of the bags extended over several fields. Furthermore, the manure used for fertilizing the fields was largely that of humans, with its disgusting reek. My section was lucky in that the adjacent quarry provided a certain amount of sawdust to fill sandbags required for living quarters; we also lined our sandbag walls with stone blocks. The local school children helped us with this by carrying the blocks to the section position, and eventually their elder brothers, after watching our inept efforts to build the stone walls, set to with saws and planes to build us a cook house and very high class walls. I was rather worried as to how we could recompense them for all their hard work, so I consulted the school master who said, 'If you would allow them, when they leave, to take a handful each out of your swill bins, they will feel amply rewarded.'!

The threat of any Italian air raids on the island soon became very remote and we were put on a six-hour state of readiness. We used therefore to go out each morning to our Section positions to carry out training, maintenance, and to improve our shelters. We then returned to Imtarfa in time for late lunch, leaving a guard on the Section position. An officer had to visit all four Sections of our Battery each night, which involved a round trip of almost fifty miles. Each subaltern had to do this once every four nights. My driver for these occasions was driver Webb, who arguably became the most genuine and loyal friend I have ever had. He had been a Durham coal miner until he enlisted. He was most refreshingly enthusiastic about everything to do with Army life. He was a most hardworking member of the Regimental football team and always volunteered to represent the Battery in the less popular competitions such as boxing and cross-country running. On these night drives we used to talk endlessly. Eventually he became my driver/batman.

Chinny Lindsay, Henry Walker and I bought an Austin tourer which we shared amicably, and which gave us a chance of playing golf and tennis at the Marsa Club. Once a week we used to drive into Valetta, have an excellent supper at the Union Club, and then go on to the Moulin Rouge (in bounds to officers only) to watch the cabaret and to have a drink or two.

There were no grass playing fields on the island; they were all hard 'mutty'. Our Regimental hockey team (in which I played at inside right) had a very successful season, winning the open knockout competition. I had one unique experience on the soccer field. The best teams in the Malta League used to get crowds of up to 10,000 in their stadia on Saturdays, and they used to open their gates an hour and a half before the big match. One Saturday, my Battery eleven played Malta University, before a match between Sliema and Floriana—the Maltese equivalent of Liverpool v. Everton. When we kicked off, the ground was empty, but by half time there were about 4,000 watching us and we got enthusiastic cheering (and jeering) before the match ended. It was very nerveracking!

Among the naval officers whom I met were Lord Louis Mountbatten, later to become Allied C-in-C Far East, and the last Viceroy of India as Earl Mountbatten of Burma. He spent a lot of his spare time coaching junior naval officers at polo. Then there was Lieutenant Commander Warburton-Lee, who was an outstanding games player. He received a posthumous Victoria Cross at the Battle of Narvik.

In the summer of 1936 we heard that the Regiment was to return to England. I was in fact sent home a month before the Regiment embarked, to attend a Unit Instructors course at the AA school at Biggin Hill. I left with happy memories of Malta, which included visits to the Opera House to watch a visiting operatic company from Rome, and a Battery whole holiday spent on the only sandy beaches, at Ghain Tuffiah, facing towards Gozo. Then this area was completely undeveloped; now, I hear, it is overspilling with monster concrete hotels.

Malta was aptly described as the island of Yells, Smells and Bells. In those days it was a most intriguing place, but I would not have liked to have spent more than a year there.

King George V died while we were in Malta. We attended the Proclamation Ceremony of King Edward VIII at the Citadel, and afterwards we had drinks at the Royal Malta Regiment Mess. The Regiment's CO called for silence and said, 'I have the honour for the first time in this Colony to propose this toast. Gentlemen, King Henry VIII!' We drank the toast!

7

Lichfield and Manorbier 1937

On arrival in England, I enjoyed ten days leave at Kingsmere. I bought a second hand Morris saloon; it had four doors and electrically operated screen wipers and trafficators. The latter consisted of illuminated lever arms which went to the horizontal from their housings on either side of the car between the two doors.

I duly attended my course at Biggin Hill, and got the grading 'recommended for a Gunnery Staff Course after further experience'. I then collected Whisky from Kingsmere, and we set off for Whittington Barracks, Lichfield. The Regiment had arrived there ten days previously. To our great regret Freddy Morgan had been replaced and our new Battery Commander was Lieutenant Colonel Jocelyn Pollock. We were just in time to get organised and to carry out a fortnight's practice camp at Weybourne in Norfolk. We acquitted ourselves quite well, and we enjoyed our fortnight there.

Whittington Barracks we shared with the Depot of the South Staffordshire Regiment and the 1st Battalion of the King's Shropshire Light Infantry. The Barracks had a great deal to offer: excellent sports grounds, squash and tennis courts, and a very high class golf course just outside the barrack gates. Our Officers Mess was very comfortable.

All the subalterns who returned from Malta had four years service, and when a batch of second lieutenants were posted to us to make up numbers, I and my contemporaries were horrified at how their sense of priorities appeared to be completely different from the ones we had upheld for the last four years. We had all lived very economically and spent our savings on hunting, buying good saddlery, taking part in games and having one night out per week. The newcomers—four years junior to us—spent their money on tarting up their rooms, buying comfortable armchairs, providing their own curtains and pansy eiderdowns. It all seemed very queer to us!

The winter passed pleasantly enough. Occasional visits to

Birmingham punctuated our normal routine. I managed to fit in about four days hunting with the South Atherstone and the Meynell, though I cannot for the life of me remember whose horse I borrowed. One of our senior subalterns had a horse-box trailer for two horses and he very kindly allowed me, when I could get a horse, to share it. We played a great deal of golf, squash and tennis, and I played a lot of hockey, at which our neighbours, the KSLI, were the holders of the Army Championship.

We heard in the spring that the Regiment had been ordered to provide Depot Batteries at two Practice Camps for the whole summer, at Weybourne and at a brand new one at Manorbier, on the Pembrokeshire coast near Tenby. Polly and the Battery Commander of the other Battery were summoned one day to the CO's office. They were told to spin a coin for choice of which Practice Camp they would run. That toss and another one which took place a year later in Egypt were both most vital to me. Polly won this toss, and chose Manorbier.

Polly appointed me as Camp Staff Officer and so, early in May, he and I, accompanied by the Battery Sergeant Major, the BQMS, Gunner Webb, and Whisky, departed in our two cars, a staff car, and a lorry, and a three-ton lorry, and drove down to Manorbier. We arrived there on a glorious spring afternoon. There was a beautiful carpet of bluebells covering the whole cliff-top site of what was to be a tented camp for the Depot Battery, the permanent Gunnery Staff, and the two-at-at-time Territorial Army Practising Regiments. The views were breath-taking out to sea, with Caldey Island just peeping round the corner opposite Tenby. We chose a beautiful site for our Battery Officers Mess on a small promontary between a steep-sided little circular bay called Skrinkle Haven and the cliffs which went straight for about half a mile. The top of these cliffs were of course to be the gun positions.

Our advance party arrived next day and prepared the Battery's camp; the Battery arrived two days later to pitch the whole camp. It really seemed a shame to pitch all the marqees and bell tents on such a wonderful beauty spot.

One of my first jobs was to visit all the neighbouring farms to establish friendly relations, and to invite them and various dignitaries from Penally and Tenby to a lunch in our Battery Mess before the first Practising Regiments arrived. It was very hard work, but we were ready in ample time for the arrival of the equipment and the Gunnery Staff, and subsequently for the TA Regiments.

It proved to be a wonderful summer in all respects, and we all enjoyed it to the full. My two junior subalterns were Tony Hulton and 'Bernard' Shaw. We soon found our way to Tenby tennis club, where we were made welcome by the Honorary Secretary who, amongst other kindnesses, allowed us to have occasional hot baths in his beautiful flat. It was at the tennis club that I first met Joane Mathias-Thomas. She was away acting as reserve for the Welsh Ladies golf team at the international meeting. She duly arrived after we had been there a week and from that day on she and I got on famously. My first game of golf against her took place on the lovely Tenby links, half of which, it transpired, was owned by Joane's father, who was the leading solicitor in Tenby. Looking back on this first match, after a gap of many years, we have been unable to agree on its result. We both remember that Joane sank an indecently long putt on the eighteenth green. I maintain that it saved her from defeat, whereas she claims that it gave her victory!

The Battery's main task was to ensure that the practising units were made comfortable, that the guns and instruments were well maintained and to carry out the chores of the camp. In addition, each Monday we had to carry out a demonstration shoot for the incoming regiment. But we had no responsibility for the visiting units' firing. The Gunnery Staff were entirely responsible for this. During the first fortnight the unforgivable happened; a round burst in front of the aircraft towing the target. The gun position had RT contact with the pilot. The infuriated pilot's transmission was memorable: 'What the hell, don't you sods know that we're not pushing the target, we're pulling it!'

Colonel Pollock and his wife, a West End theatrical dancer, were a charming couple. Thanks to some excellent cocktail parties we became very popular with the inhabitants of Tenby at all levels. The district had not known any Regular Army units since the Great War, and the extent to which they took us to their hearts can best be illustrated by two stories concerning the excellent Gunner Webb, who despite his broad Geordie accent was a very personable young man.

One night I took Joane to the Tenby dance hall, and I did notice that Webb was also entertaining a girl there. Next morning when he called me with my mug of tea, I thought I heard him make a most un-Webblike remark. Thinking that I had misheard it I asked him to repeat it. He did.

'What did you think of the solicitor's daughter last night, sir?'

'How dare you, Webb!'

'Sorry, sir, I didn't mean your solicitor's daughter, I meant mine.'

A month or so later, through Joane, I received a very 'county' invitation to a Ball in north Pembrokeshire, to celebrate the coming of age of the hostess's son and heir. Three days before the event, Gunner Webb came up to me and said, 'Excuse me, sir, will you be going to the Lord-Phillips's Ball on Friday?'

I said, 'Yes, why?' to which he replied, 'Oh hell, I was going to ask if I could borrow your evening tail coat.' He had also received an invitation, I wished I had had two! They were wonderful days.

After a few weeks another detachment from our Regiment arrived down to run a non-firing TA camp at Penally, between us and Tenby. The party was commanded by Major Frank Dearden, a Scottish rugger international, and included Chinny Lindsay, Chetwynd-Stapleton (Jitters), and Charles McFeteridge. They and I, together with Joane and her very nice friends, had most enjoyable picnics, excursions, dances, cinemas, golf and tennis. The weather too was lovely, all very romantic.

One afternoon, just before the Tenby tennis tournament took place, Chinny, Jitters and I were knocking up, waiting for Joane and others to arrive, when a man arrived and asked whether he might make up our four. We readily agreed. He seemed to be a bit good! and after three games he disclosed his identity—Herman David, a member of our Davis Cup team. Joane had told me about him. He had married the elder sister of one of Joane's best friends. It then became Jitters' turn to serve and in an effort to hit his first serve to Herman David rather harder than he was capable of doing he hit too soon, and the top edge of his racquet just made contact with the bottom of the ball, which went up a considerable height with a lot of back spin on it, and just lobbed over the net. David got nowhere near the ball and Jitters cried triumphantly, 'I've aced a Davis Cup player!'

In addition to the open Tournament, the Club had a special mixed knockout tournament for the Coronation Cup; King George VI was crowned that summer. I was paired with an ageing spinster who was quite the steadiest player I had ever played with, and eventually we came out the winners of the Cup. After the war, a friend of Joane's spotted the Cup in a pawnbroker's window and sent it to me, as the first winner!

Romance was in the air; it had struck Joane and me and also Gunner Webb and the girl he eventually married the following year (not the solicitor's daughter!). Furthermore, a family from St. Clears who owned a pedigree golden retriever bitch asked if I'd allow Whisky to sire her puppies. When the time came, Whisky and the bitch spent the night together, under Webb's watchful eye, in one of our guest tents. This proved a great success. Bernard Shaw bought one of the pups, but sadly it was stolen from Whittington Barracks soon after we returned there.

We were all very sad to leave in September to return to Lichfield. We had done our job well and received wonderful friendliness and hospitality.

Whittington Barracks seemed very dull after the delights of Tenby. For the last two summers I had played no cricket of any consequence, so any hopes I may have had of getting into the Gunner Representative Eleven had now vanished. So I was not unduly disappointed when soon after Christmas my Battery was ordered to join another Regiment to go out to Alexandria. Of course I was very disappointed that it would cut off my courtship of Joane, but we agreed to write to each other frequently. The day the news broke that a lot of us were to go out to Egypt, I was sitting at dinner next to a junior subaltern named Waring. He was a most curious person; his only hobby seemed to be to sit in his quarter tapping a drum, a leather collar box and tumblers of water with drumsticks, while playing incessantly records of all the best jazz bands. He turned to me and said, 'You are lucky to be going out to Alexandria.'

Rather doubtfully I asked, 'Why?'

'Willie Lewis is out there.'

'I don't think I know him.' I said.

'No, he's a very famous band leader. Would you like me to write out something about his band for you?'

I thanked him very much. Two days later I was presented with a very well got up manuscript: 'Willie Lewis's Band' by J.H. Waring. It started: 'In the United States, this band is rated very highly. Outside America, it is by far the best.' It went on to give the history and particular merits of each of the twenty or so members of the band. When eventually we reached Alex, Chinny and I found the club in which this paragon of jazz was playing. We invited Willie Lewis to come over and have a drink with us during the interval. We showed him Waring's magnum opus; he was delighted with it and asked if he could show it to the rest of the band. They all signed it, except two who could not write their own names. I duly sent the book back to Waring, expecting him to be delighted, but I never even got an acknowledgement. Whether he thought we were pulling his leg, or whether it was lost in the post, I do not know. Needless to say, all the members of the band were negroes.

Gunner Webb, who had got engaged to his Tenby girl, was not included in the Battery for Egypt. I will therefore take the opportunity to conclude the Webb saga now. I had frequently offered him and had tried to persuade him to accept, promotion to Lance Bombardier, but he had always refused it. He was promoted eventually the day I left Lichfield. In 1939, just over a year later, he had reached the rank of Warrant Officer Class II as a BSM in Iceland. The last letter I got from him was written in Tenby when he was on embarkation leave for the Far East. In the letter he said, 'I know you'll be getting command of a Regiment soon; is there any chance of you applying for me to be your Regimental Sergeant Major? It would be a bloody fine Regiment, wouldn't it, sir?' He sailed in the convoy which reached Singapore five days before it surrendered to the Japs. He was shipped out of Singapore in a Japanese cargo ship, locked in the hold below decks with hundreds of other POWs. The ship was torpedoed, and there were no survivors.

Now to resume the narrative. I was still in Pollock's Battery and the Regiment was commanded by Lieutenant Colonel Wilson, who had commanded Q Field Battery in 21st Field Brigade at Catterick. Jim Bannerman was Assistant Adjutant and among the subalterns were Chinny Lindsay and Henry Norman Walker. We embarked on *SS Neuralia* (a sister ship to the *Nevasa* on which Malcolm had died five years before). My father and mother came to watch us sail.

8

Egypt and the Western Desert 1938—1942

We arrived at Alexandria ten days later, after a very pleasant voyage. We were taken straight away to a tented camp at Sidi Bishr, about six miles up the coast east of Alexandria. The campsite was a piece of sandy desert which had somehow intruded into the delta area. It was just like my boyhood impression of what desert should be like. The sand was almost white in colour, very fine in texture, and deep, quite unlike the Western Desert, which I got to know so well later on. The 'sand' there was dust.

Chinny and I once again bought a second-hand Austin tourer and we soon realised that we must order a fitted cotton cover for it or the wind-blown sand would have stripped all the paint off it. There were a few forlorn-looking palm trees near the road, very bent by the wind. It really was a most uncomfortable camp site. The sand got everywhere, into one's food, chest of drawers, clothing, and even into one's bed.

We spent as much of our spare time as possible in Alexandria, which had a very good English Club—the Union Club—on the very fine waterfront of the inner harbour, the Cecil Hotel, and other good hotels, and a number of cinemas. It had a lot to offer including two race courses, one at the Sporting Club and one at the Smouha Club. Both of these clubs had golf courses within the circuit of the race courses, and the Sporting Club had many excellent tennis courts.

After a few weeks we were ordered to send two guns and the relevant gun control instruments for a newly formed Egyptian Army AA Regiment to start their training. A subaltern and an assistant instructor were to accompany the equipment and stay with it for 'at least eight weeks' to ensure that it was well maintained and also to help the Biggin Hill trained Egyptian Instructors in Gunnery to start training the Regimental Officers and NCOs.

Colonel Pollock did his stuff well and advised Colonel Wilson that I should be the subaltern to go (in view of my distinguished certificate on my first course and my report on the Unit Instructor's course!) Wilson rather favoured sending Paul Hobbs, as his brother was in 3rd RHA in Cairo. Anyhow, it was decided that the two of us should cut a pack of cards to decide who was to go. I cut the queen of spades, and Paul failed to beat it. So off I went with Sergeant Mason and a convoy of guns and lorries up the desert road to Cairo. We had our final halt at Giza to polish up the guns before going through Cairo. We also took the opportunity of photographing the convoy with the Pyramids in the background. We delivered the guns to the Egyptian Barracks at Qubri el Kubba, saw off the rest of our convoy to go back to Sidi Bishr, and then reported ourselves to 3 RHA.

3RHA, commanded by 'Bubbly' White, had only been in Abassia for under a year. Bubbly had gathered together a most talented collection of officers, not merely on the technical side, for that was a must for anyone recommended for his 'jacket', but also in sport. His second-in-command was Rae Mirlees, known then as 'The Angry Major'; the nickname was the result of his expectation never to be promoted Lieutenant Colonel, despite the fact that he had been awarded an MC in the Great War and that he had passed through Staff College—such was the blockage in senior ranks caused by the large number of Regular Commissions granted towards the end of World War I. He was an ex-Army Golf champion and a good polo player. He was however saved by World War II and eventually deservedly retired as a Major General, whereas Bubbly ended the war as a Flight Lieutenant in the Observer Corps! Keith Dunn commanded D Battery. He had commanded Y Field Battery of 21st Field at Catterick; I vividly remembered that when I had said farewell to him before I left Catterick, he had told me that if I had a chance to do so I should take up polo, 'as you obviously have a good eye for a ball and you ride well enough'. That was high praise from an ex-Chief Instructor of the Equitation School, whose standards were particularly high!

Among the Captains were Friz Fowler who was an all-England polo player, and Tock Elton who was also a very high-class polo player and a very good all-round games player—he later transferred to the 8th Hussars and was killed in action. Then there was Ted Hunt, who captained the Irish rugger fifteen for several years; he was killed in Hong Kong. The subalterns included C.P. Hamilton (Ham), whom I knew very well from Gunner cricket; he was also British Amateur Squash Champion and an international hockey player. He was a very studious batsman and he and the two Reggies, Hudson and Hewtison, were automatically 1, 2, and 3 in the Gunner, Army, and Combined services Elevens. In fact, when Ham was on leave in 1938, he and Reggie Hudson made the highest first wicket stand against the Australian touring team during the whole of their tour. In 1939, in an inter-unit match in Cairo, Ham for once 'went mad', and the headlines in the Egyptian Mail next day read, 'Hamilton's Hurricane Hitting'. Ham was very proud of this and bought several copies of the paper to send to his friends at home. I would like to think that he had a copy in his breast pocket when he was killed in Eritrea the following year. Peter Hobbs was the current Army rugger captain; he and his brother Paul were both killed in the Western Desert, and Jimmy James, another hockey international, was killed in Burma. I mention these facts to bring home to the younger generations what a waste of human life a world war causes.

Before my eight weeks were up, I was sent for by General Marshal-Cornwall, the Chief of the Mission to the Egyptian Army, who told me that the Mission was to be increased by two more Instructors in gunnery (one in Field and the other in AckAck) and he would like to appoint me as Captain IG. Of course I was delighted. It meant that I would receive pay as a captain, plus an increment as a 'qualified' instructor, plus a daily allowance of £1 -10 - 0 paid by the Egyptian Government, whereas I was living in 3 RHA Mess for about 3/6 (18p). In addition, as in theory I was to be paid by the Foreign office, I received Diplomatic Corps privileges. These were most valuable as anything I bought in bulk was duty-free; for example a case of champagne I could get at 7/- a bottle! I had a special card which allowed me to buy petrol at half price at the pumps. I also had Corps Diplomatique number plates on my car. This almost caused me to get into serious trouble, because at one guest night I told Terence O'Brien Butler that now I could do no wrong in my car. So after dinner, he and three other subalterns piled into my car and we went into Cairo. There, Terence said, 'There is a one-way street; go up it the wrong way.' Meekly I obeyed; an Egyptian policeman waved his arms in horror and then, when he saw my number plate, sprang to attention and saluted. The subalterns were very impressed and so I repeated the performance down three other one-way streets with the same result. Two mornings later, I came down to breakfast to find a confidential letter covered in red seals awaiting me. I opened it and found that it was signed by the great Sir Thomas

Russell Pasha, the head of the Cairo police. It said , 'On the evening of—, your chauffeur was observed driving down the following streets in the incorrect direction. It would be much appreciated if you instructed him not to do such a thing again.' I thanked my lucky stars, as I knew full well that he must have known, from the police reports, that it was I who was driving, with a carful of slightly merry officers. So I replied by thanking him for his letter, apologising for the incident, saying that I had sacked my driver and promising that no such incident would happen again. I heard no more.

I very much enjoyed my work. I had been allotted an Egyptian Army staff car and my own driver (Mohamed Gabr). Each day I visited the Regiment's CO, the Commandant of the AA school, often the CRA Zaidy Pasha and probably the Mission HQ to report to my immediate boss—Lieutenant Colonel Bicknell. My Arabic improved rapidly, to such an extent that I could understand when an officer was teaching incorrectly. It was all slightly frustrating because I had no executive powers. If something was going wrong, I used to rush to the Battery Commander's office, where etiquette dictated that I had to drink at least one cup of coffee before starting to talk 'shop'. Generally speaking, I had the greatest respect for the junior Egyptian officers. The large gap educationally between them and their NCO's and men made them far more self-assured than their British counterparts and they were very keen to do well. The senior officers, generalising again, were very lazy and very difficult to dislodge from their offices to watch any training.

Gabr proved to be an extremely smart young man, but a hopelessly bad driver. As a result, I got permission to drive myself with Gabr sitting next to me. We did this for about three months, before reversing our roles. From that day he drove splendidly, his reactions in any circumstances seemed to be exactly the same as mine, except in one respect: if a jay walker tried to commit suicide by walking in front of the car, my instinct was to call the offender an 'ebn Hommar' (the son of a donkey), whereas Gabr used to aim a very accurate spit at the offender—far more effective!

My leisure was spent mostly at the wonderful Gezira Club on an island in the Nile. I watched a lot of polo and played some most enjoyable hockey for the club, and had by far the two best cricket seasons of my life. Matting wickets seemed to suit me and I made a large number of high scores, which got most flatteringly reported in the two English language papers. The highlight of each cricket season (1938 and 1939) was a tour of Martineau's team in April. His teams included among others four England test captains—A.P.F. Chapman, R.E.S. Wyatt, B.H. Valentine and F.R. Brown—some South African test players, and always the current captains of Oxford and Cambridge. The touring teams were so well entertained during their four week tours that by the time the 'test match' was played, they found it difficult to do their reputations justice and often lost these matches. I played against them for the Army in 1938, and in 1939 for the Army, for Combined Services Middle East and for All Egypt. This was the last time I saw Roger Winlaw who was then captain of Cambridge, as he was killed in a wartime flying accident. His Oxford counterpart—Walker—was also killed in the war.

I managed to get three weeks home leave in the summer of 1938, which coincided with Dick's holidays, immediately before he went to the RMA Woolwich. I went up to Woolwich with Dick and waited for him outside his Company office while he went in for his interview. I was rather taken aback when a Guards Sergeant Major came up to me and said, 'Have you been in to see your Company Commander yet, sir?' He was very apologetic when I answered, 'Yes, Sergeant Major, eight years ago!'

Dick had distinguished himself in his last year at Winchester by winning the senior steeplechase.

I thoroughly enjoyed my leave. I had travelled home with Donald Mackenzie, who had been at Winchester with me and was now in the Cameron Highlanders. We departed from Alexandria on a Lloyd Trestino liner, which took us to Venice, where we had twelve hours to spare before catching our train. After an exhausting morning sight-seeing we were relaxing in St. Marks's square drinking chianti, when a man came up to us. One of us must have been wearing an Old Wykehamist tie. He introduced himself as being also an OW, and insisted on giving us lunch which of course included lots more chianti. Afterwards he insisted on showing us Michelangelo's paintings in the Doge's palace. These, as we should have known, were painted on the ceilings. Gazing up at them, having imbibed far too much, nearly caused Donald and me to disgrace ourselves! We caught our train and travelled third class all the way to Le Havre and then by ferry to Southampton. The return fare was £26.

I spent Christmas 1938 and New Year's Day at Luxor and Aswan respectively with Scott Moncrief, his fiancée and her chaperone. They got engaged on New Year's Eve, despite Scotty having made a fool of himself that morning. We decided to have a game of golf at Aswan Golf Club and were advised to hire donkeys to ride to the club. On the way, Scotty started to show off demonstrating some polo shots. The donkey took exception to this, reared up, and broke his girth. Scotty finished up underneath the donkey, which then departed for home at high speed. We all enjoyed our holiday very much—the sight-seeing, the luxurious hotels and everything.

At about that time, there was a change of government in Egypt, Nahas Pasha replacing Mohamed Mahmuh Pasha, and this looked like terminating my job on the Military Mission. I then received two other offers, both extremely good ones. First I got a letter from Uncle Harry, who had recently been appointed Governor of the United Provinces in India, asking me if I would like to go out there as his Military ADC. The other was from Keith Dunn, who said he had persuaded Bubbly White to ask for me to fill a vacancy for a subaltern in D Battery RHA. I wrote to my father concerning Uncle Harry's offer, and his answer was: 'There is going to be a war, and if you spend it carrying your aunt's fur coat around India, I'll cut you off with a shilling'! So that was that! I told Keith Dunn that I should be greatly honoured if he would accept me into D Battery. In due course the War Office agreed. Meanwhile Mohamed Mahmoud ousted Nahas from office, and my appointment with the Mission was once more secure.

Meanwhile, my Egyptian Regiment had received all its 3 inch guns and had had two very successful Practice Camps at Mersa Matruh, attended by all the Egyptian VIPs: King Farouk, the Prime Minister, the Commander in Chief, and of course the Head of our Mission, General Marshal-Cornwall. Morale was therefore very high. One weekend I was invited by Zaidy Pasha to accompany him and a party of Egyptian officers to Siwa Oasis, some 150 miles south-west of Matruh and close to the Libyan border. We went in open Ford trucks, and on the way across the desert I was shown the sport of gazelle snatching. On finding a gazelle, the idea was to tire it out by making it go faster than normal by driving alongside it for a mile or two. Suddenly its stamina would flag and someone in the rear of the truck would then put his arm over the animal's back and under its belly and lift it bodily into the back of the truck. As soon as the gazelle recovered from the shock and was breathing normally again it was released, and the graceful animal cantered off to rejoin its friends. Siwa Oasis was huge and most interesting. As well as having springs it had a number of artesian wells. A remarkable place considering there was nothing but rocky, dusty desert within 120 miles of it.

My father and mother came out to Egypt early in 1939. They stayed in a hotel in Cairo and I showed them all the local sights. While they were there, they had a good view of the arrival of the Shah of Persia's sister to become betrothed to King Farouk. As part of the celebrations there was a big parade of the Egyptian Army at Almaza, attended by the King and his fiancée. My parents and I had front row seats in the Royal Enclosure. Dear old Zaidy Pasha embarrassed me rather by introducing my father to VIPs as 'Haig's Daddy'!

I went down to Sidi Bishr one weekend to say farewell to my old Regiment. I had a final 'night out' with Chinny and Henry Walker. It was the last time I was destined to see either of them as Chinny Lindsay was killed in Italy and Henry at Arnhem. But we had a great farewell party. On the way down on the Desert Road my car suddenly started overheating and making increasingly awful noises. Finally the engine seized up completely. The cause was not hard to diagnose. The drain plug of the sump had fallen out! After a quarter of an hour a kind Egyptian stopped and asked if he could help. He agreed to tow me the 60-odd miles to the Ford garage in Alexandria. The next day I played golf against the general manager of Ford's in Alexandria. During the round I told him of my mishap and that evening he rang me up saying that a Ford truck had overturned and burnt out in the desert. First reports he had received indicated that the engine had not been damaged. If that proved correct, would I like him to see whether the engine would fit inside my bonnet? Two days later my car was on the road again with considerably more horse power under its bonnet. The bonnet clips in fact had to be lengthened to allow the bonnet to close. This was all done for £12!

So life went on. In the summer of 1939, Tiny Burton, who was General Marshal-Cornwall's Military Assistant and who shared a very superior flat in Cairo's Garden City with two senior staff officers in the Mission, found that he was going to be alone in the flat for six weeks in the summer. He very kindly asked Scott-Moncrief and me to move into the flat for six weeks. We had six weeks of very high living, as Tiny was an extremely sociable man. His dinner parties became very well known. He used to scan the social columns of *The Sphinx* and if any celebrities were paying short visits to Cairo he used to invite them to dinner parties. The previous season, one of his guests had been Barbara Hutton, the American heiress! We held a dinner party to welcome our General back from his home leave. One of the other guests was an American lady who had only arrived in Cairo the previous day and who, Tiny said, had a very high reputation in the States as a fortune teller. We had, as usual, an excellent dinner and afterwards this woman agreed to tell people's fortunes. She made it clear that everything she would say ignored what might happen in the war, which now appeared inevitable. After a time, she was persuaded to tell Marshal-Cornwall's fortune. She studied his hands for a long time and then made one or two fairly ordinary comments such as 'I see that you and your wife have recently returned from a holiday in Scotland', and then she said, 'I see that you have a daughter at school in Switzerland.'

The General said, 'How clever of you; in fact I have two daughters there.'

At this she studied his hand more carefully and finally said, 'I'm awfully sorry, but I've got a headache; do you mind if I stop fortune telling now.'

The General left soon afterwards and we asked the woman why she had 'dried up' on the General. She explained that his hand showed very distinctly that only one of his daughters was in Switzerland, and she did not know what to do or say. The very next morning news was cabled out that his eldest daughter had died suddenly the day before. A psychic phenomenon, if ever there was one.

On the lighter side, one evening Fatty Frewen and I were invited by Prince Ismael Daoud to dine with him at Madame Badia's nightclub at Giza. It was an interesting, if not delicious, dinner, and afterwards we went to the Royal Box to watch cabaret. In the interval, Madame Badia came up to the Royal Box and was introduced to everyone. After asking the Prince—he was the King's uncle—if he would like to request any special song for her to sing, she also said that perhaps the British officers would like also to request a song. I looked blankly at Fatty, who eventually asked for a song called 'Hassan'. Badia's face dropped, and she told the Prince that she would have to get permission from a policeman before she could sing that. However, she went back on stage and got a great ovation after singing the Prince's request. She then said that for an encore, at the special request of the British officers in the Royal Box and with the prior permission of the police, she was going to sing 'Hassan'.

The audience went into raptures, cheered and clapped, looking up at us and giving us lecherous winks. She started to sing, and every time she came to the 'punch-line', which of course was quite above our heads and equally obviously very lewd, most of the audience turned to look at us. I was blushing like a beetroot and even Fatty was a bit disconcerted; he started to apologise to the Prince, saying that he had not realised it was *that* kind of song. The Prince said that he knew it, and that the request had made his evening.

During the war, Madame Badia was awarded the OBE. Her nightclub was in bounds to Other Ranks and she, besides singing and belly-dancing (no mean feat for a woman in her late sixties), kept order considerably better than any Regimental Sergeant Major could have done!

On September 3rd we all sat in the Officers Mess at midday to hear Neville Chamberlain's speech declaring that we were now 'at war' with Germany. We listened to it with silver pint tankards of champagne (duty-free by courtesy of me) in our hands. It makes me very sad to think back to that occasion and to realise how few of us managed to survive the war.

I was promoted Major, and was sent down to Alexandria to advise the Egyptian Brigadier who was in charge of the Anti Aircraft defences there. I took up residence in the Beau Rivage Hotel, near Sidi Bishr. I was very comfortable there and enjoyed myself almost as much as in Cairo. I played a lot of golf at Smouha and a bit of cricket for Alexandria Cricket Club. Gabr of course came with me and we covered big mileages siting and visiting gun positions, and searchlight and Bofors positions. I felt that I now had considerably more executive power.

Towards the end of October, one evening I went into the bar at the Beau Rivage to find Frank Dearden there. He was second in command of 9th HAA (Supplementary Reserve) Regiment RA. This Regiment started recruiting a week or two before the outbreak of war and was up to strength within a week. It was recruited entirely in Londonderry and North Antrim. The CO was appointed; he selected his Battery Commanders and Adjutant, who then formed a selection committee to select officers, warrant officers and NCOs, and to distribute the rest of the volunteers to Regimental HQ and to the Batteries. The whole Regiment was shipped out to Alexandria to get organised and to take over 3.7 inch AA guns, with a view to taking over the air defence of Alexandria with my Egyptians. When this

Regiment arrived in Sidi Bishr, although the war had started, ordinary peacetime procedures were still in force in Alexandria. One of the Battery Captains, Sammy Haughton, who had held a commission in the 1914-18 war, found himself as Regimental Field Officer of the Day. He was the son of a very wealthy landowner in County Antrim. In the small hours of the night he buckled on his sword and went to the Camp's main gate. He was correctly challenged by the sentry and he correctly answered 'Visiting Grand rounds'. The sentry ordered, 'Turn out the Guard'; everything was going well and Sammy's confidence was growing. The Guard turned out reasonably quickly, with the exception of one man who had obviously got into a complete muddle. He eventually emerged from the Guard tent, went straight up to Captain Haughton, peered up at his face and on recognising him said, 'Oh, thank the Lord, it's only you, Master Sammy; hold on a moment and I'll go and get m' gun!' He turned out to be one of Sammy's father's gamekeepers. I tell this story to illustrate the unique spirit of this wonderful Regiment, which many years later I had the honour to command. One of the Battery Commanders was Sir Basil McFarland, who had been a rugger international and was the current mayor of Londonderry. I had a most sociable time showing Frankie and Basil round the night life of Alexandria!

During this curious period of 'phoney war' I was invited by John Innes, who was on the staff of Barclay's Bank DC & O to move into the Bank flat, as all the occupants except him had left to join the forces. It was a lovely flat overlooking the Sporting Club and had an excellent staff. We lived very well, and thanks to John I got involved in the more social side of Alexandria. I had two girl friends whose first names I have forgotten; one turned out to be the sister of the infamous Philby who was convicted of spying against the Allies; the other's surname was Bogdadli. She was a very cosmopolitan girl and spoke fluent English, French, Arabic, Greek, and Italian! Her father was president of the Sporting Club and when the tennis tournament took place there just before the outbreak of war, I was invited to sit at the high table at the pre-tournament dinner. The chief guest was the current Wimbledon champion—Baron von Cram. We met for drinks before going into dinner, and Miss Bogdadli introduced me to the VIP thus:

'Baron von Cram. meet my friend Earl Haig.'

The Baron clicked his heels and bowed stiffly. I was furious with her! A year or so later when I was on leave from the Western Desert I met her again. By then the family had changed its name from Bogdadli to Bentley!

Then, in the summer of 1940, with the British evacuation at Dunkirk and the increasing bombing of England, the Italians declared war, and at last our war ceased being 'phoney' and became real. I was sent out to Mersa Matruh with an Egyptian HAA Regiment and an LAA Battery for the air defence of Matruh, which was our rail-head in the Western desert. We were the only AA defences west of Alexandria. Matruh garrison was commanded by a Brigadier Selby—a New Zealander—and the garrison consisted of a British Infantry Brigade plus a little more. Brigadier Selby, with the approval of the CO of my Egyptian Regiment, treated me as his air defence commander. Our problems were considerable. We had no system of early warning of air raids; radar had not reached the Western Desert! The Italian Savoya aircraft were faster than the gladiators which were the only fighters available, and the Italian planes dropped their bombs from a height of 20,000 feet, which was about the maximum height at which our 3 inch guns were at all effective.

As luck would have it, we had in our westernmost gun position a most remarkable man—an ombashi (corporal) who was possessed of most remarkably keen hearing and phenomenal eyesight. He was permanently on duty throughout the hours of daylight, although the manual said that no 'spotters' should be on duty for more than two hours at any time! He sat in a bell tent, and long before anyone else could hear an aircraft, he would hear it. He then dashed to his identification telescope in time for his section commander to identify the plane as hostile (a fairly safe bet), and then ran to the predictor and the height finder, and got them on target long before it was visible to the normal human eye. The result was that never did we fail to engage an enemy raid as soon as it came within range. Before the Egyptian unit left Matruh, Brigadier Selby recommended the ombashi for a medal. He was awarded an MBE.

I do not think we claimed any Savoyas as definitely brought down by our gun fire, but the Italians never dared come in at a lower height, and dropped their bombs prematurely as often as not, as soon as our shell bursts appeared. One night a daring Italian plane came in very low from the sea to drop leaflets on the town, exhorting the Egyptians not to help the British Army. By a great stroke of luck, a searchlight managed to hold it in its beam for just sufficiently long for an Egyptian Bofors gun to shoot it down into the lagoon. It was a wonderful effort, considering that it was the first time an enemy plane had come within range of our LAA for three months.

As soon as the first air raid occurred I moved out of Hilliers Hotel, overlooking the almost land-locked beautiful blue lagoon and the snow-white sand-dunes which guarded its narrow entrance. No wonder that Matruh was Anthony and Cleopatra's favourite holiday home! I moved on to one of our most central gun positions. The faithful Gabr appointed himself as my batman as well as being my driver. He called me in my tent and for the first two mornings he watched intently my getting-up process. Thereafter, he untucked my sandfly net, passed me my mug of tea, received it back, put my slippers on my feet before they touched the ground, produced hot water and my shaving brush with the right amount of soap, my razor, and my toothbrush with toothpaste all ready for use. We both saw the funny side of this, and shared a good laugh. He really was excellent.

After a month or two, I developed a nasty go of amoebic dysentry and spent three days in the casualty clearing station at Daaba, whilst a khamsene sandstorm raged. Visibility went down to five yards and the temperature of up to 110°F with a force 8 wind. I got back to Matruh within a week. Soon after my return Brigadier Selby sent for me and told me that the CO of the Cheshire Regiment had complained to him that the crew of an Egyptian Bofors gun sited in his Battalion area had abandoned their gun and run to their slit trenches during an air raid and at a time that enemy planes were presenting them with an ideal target for their gun. He had asked the Brigadier to order his Battalion to take over the gun. The Brigadier told me to go and investigate the incident. I did so. The raid had occured at the time that the gun detachment was being relieved by a second detachment. The relieved detachment had run to their slit trenches. The enemy planes never came below 20,000 feet and so the new gun detachment had correctly crouched under the sandbag walls of the emplacement, while the No.1 had kept a lookout for any target to come within range. I reported the facts to Brigadier Selby who said. 'I thought so', and told me to go behind a canvas partition and listen to what he had to say to the Battalion Commander. Phew!—it was worth hearing. The CO was ordered to hand over the Battalion to his second in command immediately and to catch the first train back to Alexandria, as he never wanted to see him again.

After about four months, the Egyptian units were relieved by British units and we returned to Alexandria. I received a Mention in Despatches for my services to the garrison.

Morale was very low in Alexandria. We were all desperately worried that Hitler would invade England. Mail from home was most erratic. One felt 'out of it'. After winning a Monthly Medal at Smouha, I remember writing home saying that it looked as if that would be the only medal I would get in this war! The Navy of course was very busy. I remember turning out for Alexandria Cricket Club one Saturday and finding that my usual opening partner was not playing. He was a pilot of a Walrus on one of the aircraft carriers, and the reason for his absence was that he was being de-briefed on the raid that had sunk the majority of the Italian Fleet in Taranto harbour. The Walruses flew at upper deck level down the lines of warships at anchor. They went in so low that the Italian AA guns were unable to engage them without causing much more damage and many more casualties to their own ships than to the slow lumbering Walruses busy dropping torpedoes at point blank range.

At this stage of the war it was very unusual to see anyone wearing a medal ribbon, so I was very surprised one evening when I was sitting at the bar of the Cecil Hotel with a friend. I tapped a weedy-looking Tank Corps subaltern on the shoulder and asked him to pass the chips down to us. As he did so, I saw on his chest the Victoria Cross and a Military Cross. This was Pip Gardener whom I got to know later in a prisoner of war camp.

I played golf frequently with Commander Nicholson who had already had two destroyers sunk under him, one at Narvik and one in the Mediterranean. One day he rang me up and asked me if I could make up a four at Smouha. When I turned up I found that the other two members of our four were the C-in-C Admiral Sir Andrew Cunningham, and Admiral Vian, the Admiral of the Mediterranean Destroyers! Not long after this Nicholson was promoted Captain and got command of a cruiser. This was eventually sunk when helping to evacuate our forces from Greece. I am told that as he came to the surface his first words were, 'Thank God I left my golf clubs at Smouha'!

Alexandria received frequent heavy raids by German and Italian bombers, always at night. Round the periods of nights when the moon was full, I used to spend the nights on various gun positions and I became very proud of my Egyptian gunners. One day we moved a section of guns right into the dockyard area. They dug their guns in and dug slit trenches for the relief detachments, but had not had time to revet the trenches. As bad luck would have it, a land mine was dropped on the slit trenches, and twenty-five soldiers were killed. I spent the next night on this gun position, and when the raid started I greatly admired the way the Section carried out its duties, apparently without a thought as to what had happened the previous night.

I got a week's leave in the winter of 1940 and went to Cairo, where I met Lionel Lewin, who was recovering from a terrible head wound. By then he had got an MC and bar. We decided to have three nights in Upper Egypt at Luxor and Aswan. It was a most enjoyable and invigorating leave.

It was not until August 1941 that my request to leave the Military Mission to play a more active part in the war bore fruit. I had been on the Mission for three and a half years, and in that time I had made many friends among the Egyptian officers, so I had a great number of farewells to make. When Gabr delivered me for the last time to my flat, we had a most emotional parting. He was the only Egyptian with whom I conversed entirely in Arabic; all the officers preferred speaking to me in English. I had bought a gold watch to give Gabr in recognition of the devoted service he had given me for over three years. He was overcome with gratitude and, after we had exchanged traditional Arabic goodbyes, he turned to my successor and said, 'What time I come for you tomorrow?' I was amazed as I had never heard him attempt a word of English before; I congratulated him heartily in Arabic and he drove away grinning but with tears pouring down his cheeks.

I flew to Haifa the next day to join the Staff Course at the Staff College. I was two days late arriving. When I reported to the Commandant, General Dorman Smith, he greeted me, I thought rather unkindly, with the words, 'Ah, Haig, I'm glad you've decided to give up your neutrality at last'. I met several old friends on the course, including Lionel Lewin and George Baker. It was a splendid course and a most interesting one. It lasted three and a half months and I learnt just as much from my fellow students as I did from our instructors. We worked long hours. Occasionally in the evenings we went down from Mount Carmel to Haifa and visited one or two bars. Every bar seemed to have its own German or Austrian Jewish refugee as its musician. They were all most talented instrumentalists. They never stopped playing and were only too pleased to play any requests whether classical or jazz.

We had a three-day break halfway through the course. Lionel, Ray Leaky and I went in his car to Jerusalem, Bethlehem, Petra, Jerash, and Amman, and to one or two crusader castles in Jordan. Ray was in the Tank Corps. He had been in Tobruk, which was still under siege. He had got bored doing nothing, as there was not a real role for tanks within the perimeter, so he was loaned to an Australian Infantry Battalion, whose CO recommended him after an infantry skirmish for a Victoria Cross. While we were at Haifa he heard that he had not been awarded the VC but only a bar to his MC.

Another feature of the course was a battlefield tour of the landings in Syria and the defeat of the French in Syria. Again with Lionel and Ray, I visited Beirut, the Cedars of Lebanon and Damascus before returning to Haifa.

At the end of the course I was appointed Brigade Major of the AntiAircraft Brigade of the Western Desert.

After a few days in Alexandria to organise my somewhat scattered possessions, I caught a train to Mersa Matruh, booked in at the transit camp and tried to organise transport to take me on to Barce, where my headquarters had established itself following the German-Italian retreat and the abandonment of Benghazi. Fortunately that evening I met George Bastin, now a Brigadier, who had been a Captain in Sidi Bishr with me. He was on his way to take up an appointment in Benghazi and had a staff car. He gladly agreed to give me a lift the next day and drop me off at Barce.

The desert beyond Sollum was new to me. We went via Bardia, Gambut, Tobruk and Gazala to Derna. Then we climbed from the featureless desert into the hills of Jebel Ahdur (the Green Mountains). I was most surprised how beautiful it looked, with its steep valleys, its streams and shrubs and wild flowers. We eventually descended to Barce. Altogether it was a drive of about 300 miles. I found our Brigade HQ and was given a great welcome by Brigadier Stebbings, the Brigade Commander. He had commanded a Territorial AA regiment in Kent before the war and had brought the Regiment out in 1940. He had recently got command of the Brigade. In civil life he was a dentist in Broadstairs; as a TA Second Lieutenant studying medicine in a London hospital he had been on the spot in 1916 to witness the Silvertown explosions and for his bravery had been awarded the Edward Medal, now superseded by the George

Cross. He also got the MC later in the Great War. John Bowley was the Brigade Intelligence Officer and later became our Staff Captain. The Brigade had Regiments in Benghazi, Derna and Tobruk, so Stebbo and I spent a lot of time travelling, visiting our units, and liaising with the various Formations in our Area.

By March 1942 we had had to withdraw our units as the Germans had landed two more Armoured Divisions and had begun to drive eastwards again. We moved our two more advanced Regiments and our Brigade HQ into Tobruk and deployed a Regiment at Derna which was now the new railhead.

Our Brigade Headquarters were the underground shelters of an abandoned Italian AA Regiment, with their guns still in position nearby. These were busy days as the 2nd South African Division moved into Tobruk to form its garrison in the event of General Ritchie not being able to hold his Gazala line, in which case Tobruk would be besieged once more. We soon realised that we would have to get hold of the mass of survey data that must have accumulated during the first siege. The South African division were useless and failed to get the required data. Stebbo formed our HQ as a Corps CRA's HQ. That is to say that he assumed command of all the Artillery other than the Divisional Artillery and the field Regiment supporting the Indian Brigade. It was obvious that we were going to be very short of guns. The landward perimeter of the defences was about 28 miles in length and we only had one Medium Regiment. We had therefore to be prepared for our AA regiments to be capable of augmenting the ground defensive fire, and at worst the anti-tank defences for which the Divisional Anti-Tank Regiment was the only specialist regiment. Nobody could tell us even where the minefields exactly were. It was an unbelievable confusion which the 2 SA Division was incapable of solving. For our part, we sent urgent requests to GHQ Cairo for dial sights and anti-tank sights for our AA guns.

Just prior to our move back to Tobruk, a WOI Artillery clerk was posted to our HQ. He was a very pleasant man, but he had never before been in a combatant HQ, most of his time having been spent at Woolwich with RA Records, so Operation Orders, March Tables and such-like were closed books to him. I tried hard to be tactful with him, but I had to have my drafts of the Orders for our withdrawal to Tobruk retyped several times, as he had used unauthorised abbreviations and committed several other sins which would have brought the wrath of General Ritchie's HQ upon us. The same thing happened again with my Operation orders concerning the AA regiments in Tobruk accepting a Medium Artillery and Anti-Tank role. His opinion of me and mine of him were at a low ebb when, the day before we were finally besieged, he bounced into my office waving the last copy of the *Egyptian Gazette* to reach us, smiling all over his face. He put it down in front of me and pointed to the column headed 'Answers to Sporting Correspondents'. Somebody had asked what the Lawrence Trophy was presented for. The answer correctly stated that it was an annual trophy presented to the scorer of the fastest century during the first-class cricket season in England. It went on to mention some of the great people who had won it—Frank Woolley, Duleepsinji, etc., and finally, for no good reason, finished by saying, 'The fastest century ever recorded in Egypt was made by Captain A.E.G. Haig at Gezira in 1938.'

'Was this you, sir?' he asked triumphantly, and from then on we became the best of friends. Unfortunately he was killed within a fortnight of this, when our HQ received a heavy attack by the dreaded Stukas, the German divebombers.

On June 20th 1942 we were woken up by a heavy bombardment on the eastern sector of the perimeter, held by an Indian Brigade. All our plans having been made and put into effect, Brigadier Stebbings and I drove to Divisional HQ to find out what the situation was. General Klopper said that he considered that the attack on the Indian Brigade was a feint and that the eventual attack would be at the western end of the perimeter. The total length of the perimeter was 28 miles and was defended by a mere four Infantry Brigades, with a Guards Brigade in reserve and the remnants of a Tank regiment which had been severely mauled in the 'Cauldron' battle. We then visited all the detached HAA units which we had ordered to take on a 'Ground Role'. We had received a quantity of Polish dial sights only a few days earlier; these had been fitted to the guns and extensive training had taken place in firing in the Ground Role to augment the Medium Artillery. No anti-tank or telescopic sights had been received, nor any armour piercing shells for anti-tank shooting. So we ordered guns in the anti-tank role to use their Polish dial sights set at zero, and to fire high explosive shells set at safety; in other words, 28 pounds of metal which would not explode on impact. We then returned to our HQ to find it in a shambles as a result of the Stuka attack. John Bowley had been wounded and had driven our WOI clerk to hospital. Orders were given to evacuate our HQ and to man our reserve, which was nearer the town. Things were obviously going very badly. At about 3 p.m. General Klopper rang up to say that he hoped to counter-attack the armoured penetration on the eastern flank with our 6th Battalion RTR. He expected the attack to take place in the vicinity of our old HQ, where we had a section of guns sited among the knocked-out Italian guns. I got the Brigadier's permission to visit the section to ensure that the subalterns were confident of telling the difference between the German Mark IV tanks and our Valentines. He agreed. While I was briefing the two officers in the Command Post, we heard firing very close to us, and then the sound of the rumble of tanks. I sent one officer to each of the two guns. Sure enough, three Mark IVs came over the skyline about 400 yards in front of us. I ordered the guns to engage them. The firing raised such a cloud of dust that it was impossible for me and for the guns to observe the fire, so under cover of the dust I dashed out and found a reasonably sheltered place about twenty-five yards in front of the guns and out of the direct line of fire. From there I was able to shout corrections to the nearest gun. I then witnessed a slugging match resembling two punchdrunk heavyweight boxers exchanging blows. Our further gun was put out of action very early on, but the nearer one, commanded by Sergeant Ryan, put up a wonderful show. The tanks for some reason made no effort to move or to outflank us. I had been trying to direct the fire at the tanks' tracks, knowing that we had no hope of piercing their armour, and can only surmise that this had been successful.

An article published in the *Gunner Magazine* in August 1984 quoted from a book by Herr Hackman about Rommel's war. Concerning Rommel's capture of Tobruk, he wrote, 'One 3.7 AA gun position held up the attack of 5 Panzer Regiment, destroying four tanks, until the detachments were overrun.'

I saw one of our layers killed or wounded, and then another; finally Sergeant Ryan layed the gun himself. How long this queer contest lasted, I do not know. Eventually our gun was put out of action and I told the subalterns to destroy their guns by putting a round down the end of the barrel and firing a round into it. We then sorted out the wounded and evacuated the position. I went back to where I had left my car; the driver had departed and the car would not start, so I started to walk and run back across the barren wastes of the Gubbi landing ground. The only cover consisted of the line of telegraph poles along the road, and the cemetery of those killed in the first siege. It was while going through this that I was knocked over by a shell burst; on opening my eyes I saw a wooden cross with RIP on it. I soon realised that it was not an instruction to me, and got to my feet, only for my field glasses to fall to the ground; the strap that held them round my neck had been cut! Anyhow, I got back all right, and the Brigadier and I paid another visit to Divisional HQ. Our tank counter-attack never took place as all the tanks except two were still in REME workshops!

One of the other troops of the Brigade had distinguished itself against a tank attack. It was commanded by Tim Toppin, who was eventually awarded a Military Cross.

As far as I could make out, no redeployment of our defending forces took place that evening, nor was planned for the next morning. No counter attack took place. When Rommel continued his attack next morning, it was not surprising that his armoured divisions soon broke right through the eastern sector, where the Indian Brigade had put up stiff resistance. The surrender took place that morning. No part of the 2nd South African division had fired a shot in anger, and the Guards Brigade had not been committed into the battle. It was total disgrace. No wonder General Klopper was tried after the war. His whole HQ was a shambles, suffering from friction between the Anglos and the Boers.

I have described subsequent events in my Prisoner of War Diary, anyhow up to our move to Marish Trubau in December 1943, so I will resume my recollections at that point.

Capture and Journey to Italy

The Brigadier and I drove up to HQ 2nd South African Division at about 10 a.m. on Sunday June 21st.

A dirty white flag was flying over the General's dugout. As we were getting out of our staff car, another car drove up, containing a South African staff officer, a dust-covered, tall, poker-faced major of the 21st Panzer Division. Together they went down into General Klopper's dugout.

After discussing things with various people we realised, as indeed in our hearts we had known since the previous night when the General had decided against a 'sauve qui peut' breakout, that unconditional surrender was all that we could expect. Consequently Brigadier Stebbings and I decided to make a bolt in the car to the wadis on the coast, about two miles away across the minefields. Our plan was to hide the car away and lie up in the rocks until dark, and then try to bluff our way out of the western perimeter. We would then steer south for about twenty miles before turning east. We had enough water, petrol and food with us to do this. Eric Haunton (5 LAA Battery) joined us.

We reached the coast safely. We hid the car away in a wadi, put a camouflage net over it, and found a good hiding place for ourselves. We then washed, shaved and ate some breakfast. The Brigadier had his complete kit in the car; John Bowley's (Staff Captain) kit was there also, but none of mine was aboard as I had been 'missing' the previous afternoon when the vehicles had been packed.

We were basing our plan on the hope that the Jerries would be so overcome by the easiness and complete success of their victory that they would flock into Tobruk to loot and collect prisoners there, before bothering to round up the outliers on the more inaccessible places on the coast to the west of the town.

This hope proved entirely vain. Within an hour or two we heard German shouts and bursts of tommy gun fire. They came nearer; it was obviously a systematic 'round-up'. They spotted some people hiding within fifty yards of us. We saw them find our car and then they started spraying the rocks with tommy gun fire. It was hopeless. We eventually surrendered to two Panzer NCOs.

I had left my revolver in the back of the car. One of the Germans stayed with us by the car, while the other went off to round up some other people. Surreptitiously I went to the car and found my revolver. Our guard had his back turned and his mate was 50 yards away and out of sight. I had to decide quickly whether, if I murdered the man, we still would have a chance of escape. I did not have time to consult the others. I decided it was an unfair risk to take without the consent of the others; so I tamely destroyed my revolver as best I could against a rock. From what I saw later, fortunately for my peace of mind, I know that we would have had no chance of making a getaway, as the country between us and the road was thick with German Infantry and tanks.

We were then allowed to collect what kit we could carry. I went through John Bowley's kit and reduced it to a suitcase full, mostly of stuff that I thought would be of use to myself, as I expected John to be in the hospital; he had stopped a piece of bomb with his back when our HQ was dive-bombed the previous day. We did not, as it turned out, have far to walk before we were put on a Mk IV tank. This was lucky as my boots were in fragments after my adventures of the previous day. A particularly dirty, unpleasant-looking German private told me to give him my field glasses, which I still had hanging round my neck by their bullet-cut strap. I mumbled 'Verboten' and pointed to a Jerry officer; he threatened me with his revolver but I kept saying 'Verboten' and 'Officer' and pointing. Eventually he went and consulted the officer, and I took the opportunity of smashing the lenses; when he returned, I handed him the remnants. When he saw what I had done, he again pointed his revolver at me. I was so 'done' that I really did not worry whether or not he was going to pull the trigger. Instead however he contented himself with some remarks that sounded distinctly uncomplimentary.

The whole area was full of German tanks and MT. After a bit we were transferred to a lorry and we joined a convoy of other lorries also containing officer prisoners. We passed columns of marching ORs, mostly South Africans. Many of the 'blacks' were drunk and incapable of marching; these were shot by the Jerries and there were a number of their corpses lying by the roadside. Fires were burning everywhere. Never have I seen such a depressing sight.

We eventually arrived at Gubbi aerodrome, where we found most of the garrison already assembled in the vast cage. The sand was blowing badly. Morale was incredibly low. What a vast number of prisoners to be taken without, in the case of the majority of them, any sort of a fight.

Later in the day the Camerons marched in with their pipes playing, arms swinging and a parade ground look. The mob gave them a cheer. Late in the evening the Jerries at last produced some water. Uproar ensued. The officers and men had been segregated; everyone was extremely thirsty, and the Jerries could not control them. Stebs, very nobly, took on the thankless job of bringing order out of chaos. He got up on to a tar barrel with his shooting stick and shouted some 'home truths' (well deserved) to the assembled officers. He caused great offence to the Indian Army by referring to their men as 'niggers'. This too had the desired effect because the Indians had been the worst offenders. Luckily it was about the longest day of the year and by dark everyone had had at least a taste of water.

It was a miserable night. The Brigadier and I shared a blanket, huddling as close as we could to a group of tar barrels, which afforded slight shelter from the wind and sand. There were wild rumours that 'Strafer' Gott (13 Corps) was fighting at El Adem with a relief column.

The sandstorm continued the next day. The Germans produced us something to eat about mid-day. Afterwards, to our joy and surprise, we were told that most of the officers would start their rearward journey in the afternoon.

I was one of thirty in the trailer of a 10-ton lorry. We moved off at about 3.30 in a long convoy. The chief impression that remains with me is the very low standard of driving of all the vehicles on the road. Over half the vehicles we passed seemed to be captured British ones. Our guards were Libyan Arabs, which made the South Africans particularly angry. We got to Tmimi at about 6.30 and were told we were to spend the night there. It was a most depressing sand-blown spot, and so the Brigadier managed to persuade a German officer to take our lorry and two others on to Derna. We arrived at the top of the Derna escarpment well after dark and had a bit of difficulty in getting round some of the hairpin bends with the trailer. The leg, which we had blown when we withdrew the previous February, had not been mended, but they had taken the road along a new and steeper line. The POW camp was a broken-down fort on the far side of the town, beyond our former Brigade HQ. Here we had our first search. I had only what I stood up in, so it was all right, but other people were looted right and left. Crispin Ardern, among others, had his wristwatch taken. There were no officers present at the search. Our searchers were Italians. The German officer had apologised to us for having to hand us over to the Italians! I should have said that John Bowley had joined us that morning at Gubbi, where of course he reclaimed his suitcase, but kindly gave me a pair of desert boots. He did not however come on our convoy as he was receiving treatment when we left.

We were put into a broken down corrugated iron hut with a concrete floor. The roof was mostly conspicuous by its absence and the state of the hut was, to put it mildly, most unhygenic. There was however just room for us all to lie full length. It started to rain very heavily; fortunately I had had the foresight to choose a pitch with a sound bit of roof above it. Morale was very low and Stebs, to raise it, handed round some cigars which we had salvaged from John Bowley's kit. Just as the hundred-odd cigars were becoming stumps, who should walk in but John himself! He had followed us in another lorry. He sniffed the expensive aroma, spotted us and said, 'Ah, that's an idea, cigars! Do you know what happened to mine, Tony?' I, in a cowardly way, allowed Stebs to explain the tragic situation! The least we could do was to invite him to share our blanket and sound bit of roofing. Very soon, despite rain and rifle fire, we were enjoying some much-needed sleep.

The next morning was fine. Stebs was offered a trip in a Staff car with the 'brass hats'. He very kindly asked if I could accompany him, but that was not to be. So after giving me a pull-over, a pair of socks and a vest, he bade us farewell, to our mutual regret. Ardern very kindly presented me with a very substantial leather suitcase, a few bits of clothing, a towel, and a teaspoon, which was later to prove a most sought-after piece of kit! In twelve hours I had changed from a 'have not' to a gentleman of property.

The sentries had been very jumpy all night and for no apparent reason had fired volleys into the OR's hut. We never heard what the casualties were. After a brew of acorn coffee we were packed once more into our lorries and trailers and the convoy took the road once more. It was an uncomfortable journey as there was not room to sit down. However, I managed to lean against my suitcase. The day was fine after the night's rain; the Jebel country was looking its very lovely best.

Our destination proved to be Barce, where there was an established transit camp. We were lucky in finding there an efficient and helpful Italian staff. Within a very short time of our arrival we were given forms to fill in, official postcards to write to our next-of-kin, a blanket, a towel and a cake of soap. We were shown to one of the six wooden huts. It was closely packed with double-decker wooden beds; some of the beds already contained lice and bugs but once more I was lucky. Within a couple of hours we were given a rice stew and a tot of vino. It was a great relief to be treated more or less as an individual again instead of one of a herd of the lowest of the low cattle. It was a treat to be able to take one's boots off for the first time for four days.

The Italian Major who was the Commandant was the only Italian officer I ever met for whom I had any respect. He handled us efficiently and tactfully.

On my second evening I was accosted by someone whom I failed immediately to recognise. He proved to be Hugh Haig whom I had met at Pen I Thon in 1938. As Felix Haig was also one of our party, it meant that three of the clan had been scooped up in Tobruk.

We spent the ensuing days somehow. I remember some much-needed clothes washing, a lot of gossip, a lot of sleeping and an occasional impromptu singsong. It was after one of these that a most astonishing scene took place. It had just got dark, but there was a lovely full moon. We were strolling back to our huts when we heard a very fine tenor voice singing outside the barbed-wire perimeter. It proved to belong to one of the Bersigleri sentries. He sang very well indeed and soon upwards of three hundred officers congregated near the wire to listen. He was tremendously applauded after each song! A Bersigleri sergeant came over and tried to shut him up in the middle of a song, without success. By the end of the song, the sergeant was leading the shouts demanding 'O Sole Mio' as an encore! The evening finally ended with sergeant and sentry singing a very polished duet, with a chorus of many hundreds of officers! What a 'comic opera' scene!

The food was quite good. There was a rice stew for lunch and either tinned fish or bully for supper, with an ample supply of bread. We even had an occasional tot of vino. Time hung very heavily as there was nothing to do and space was very restricted. McStocker had managed to bring a pack of cards, so we had an occasional rubber of bridge, sitting and playing on a bed.

After about a week, they started evacuating people on the next stages of the journey. They did it very approximately in alphabetical order. Crispin Ardern was the first of our lot to leave. Two days later, my turn came. The friendly little Commandant saw us off, wishing us good luck and playing the part of the genial host seeing off his guests! He had filled us with stories of the wonderful treatment we could expect when we reached Italy; how British officers had written home for their evening 'tails' so that they could attend the Opera; how they spent their days fishing quiet streams; even how they had occasional days off 'pour chercher les femmes'! I think the little man really believed all this and would have been genuinely horrified at the reality.

We had an uneventful trip to Benghazi in lorries. The transit camp was on the western edge of the town. It consisted of huts made of the ubiquitous Italian ground-sheets. The beds too were made of ground-sheets slung on a wooden framework. My bed, being within three feet of the roof, on which the sun had been shining all day, was quite untenable by day and stifling by night. The previous two parties from Barce were still in the camp. They had twice been taken to the aerodrome, but error had crept in on both occasions.

There was a big Other Ranks camp nearby. One of our doctors visited it and was horrified at its condition. There were no sanitary arrangements, dysentry was rife, and men were dying in the open, quite unattended. He and one or two other doctors got permission to stay behind and look after the camp. I heard afterwards that they did a jolly good job of work, although all OR camps in Libya were absolute disgraces to a nation that claims to be civilised.

No-one left the next day. It was one of the most unpleasant days of my captivity: terribly hot, no shade, nothing to do and a bed uninhabitable except by bugs. The following day we were all taken to the aerodrome. We were divided into groups of about twelve, and embarked in Savoia Troop carriers, with very little fuss. Felix and Hugh were in the same plane with me. There were two pilots and a wireless operator in the forward cabin, divided from us by a sliding door. With us there were a gunner, two sentries with rifles and an Africa Corps corporal who was going on leave. We took off in turn, but did not fly in formation. We had a good view of Benghazi harbour as we were gaining height. Our demolitions of the port and breakwater did not seem to have hampered the Jerries much. There were at least three big cargo ships unloading. We climbed to about 8,000 feet, where it was terribly cold. I managed to get out my blanket, which Felix and I shared. Hugh had the lining of a Burberry to keep him from freezing. We were clad, of course in the shirt, shorts and stockings in which we had been captured. If only we had had a pilot amongst us we could quite easily have taken over the plane. The two sentries both fell asleep, the gunner was cleaning the gun in the tail and the Africa Corps man was looking out of the window. After disarming them, we could have surprised the three in the front compartment and then headed for Malta. There were no escorting fighters with us. It sounds easy and was, I believe, done successfully later on by some South African Air force officers. As it was, we had a very uneventful journey. We saw no ships, submarines or aircraft, other than the occasional one of our own convoy. We came lower as we neared the land. When we crossed the coast we got tossed about a bit, but we were so frozen by then that we were too numb to be sick!

We landed on a large grass aerodrome. I took it to be in Sicily, but subsequently learned that we were in the 'heel' of Italy—Lecce. It was a fine sight to see the planes come in one after the other and land: about thirty of them. The aerodrome looked so peaceful and so obviously untouched by the RAF that we felt very depressed and even more certain that the war in the Mediterranean was as good as over. It was a huge drome and there were vast numbers of planes, undispersed, absolutely crying out to be bombed. The RAF had never obliged.

We were taken in lorries through the broad empty streets of the town. The buildings were old. It was a nice, sleepy-looking town that had obviously seen more prosperous days. We were taken to a large building which turned out to be a tobacco factory. We were, of course, very congested, and our accommodation was only mattresses on the floor. One could not move about without treading on other people's mattresses. The rooms were clean and cool and there was plenty of air and water. Some wine and jam mysteriously appeared through the 'black market'. We had the feeling that things had taken a turn for the better, despite the fact that one saw papers acclaiming the fall of Mersa Matruh.

10

In Transit in Italy

Lili Marlene! The building was built on the four sides of a square, enclosing a dark courtyard. We were on the second floor, and from our window in the landing, across the yard, we could see the women sorting the tobacco. They came to the windows and sang 'Lili Marlene'. It was the first time I had heard it since the evening before the battle. In common with the majority of the 8th army, we used to listen to the 'blonde bombshell' singing it every night on the wireless, as the signature tune of the German propaganda hour to the British forces in North Africa.

The next morning Hugh and I found a way on to the flat roof of the building, where we had a pleasant walk, before the mob also found a way up.

At about noon we were again packed into lorries, and taken to the railway station. We were put into comfortable 2nd class carriages and were soon on our way north. The country consisted of olive groves, vineyards and terraced fields. We had a very comfortable journey—six to a carriage; it was grand to be able to sink into a cushioned seat. At one station someone shouted to some Germans on the platform, 'What do you think of the Italians?' The answer came back, 'The same as you do!'

We reached Bari the next morning, after a comfortable night. We de-trained and were told that we had 'about three kilometres' march to our camp. We quite enjoyed the prospect. To start with, our route lay through the town, reminiscent of the less clean parts of Strood! By the time we had marched three miles, my suitcase, although it was almost empty, felt like a ton weight suspended from a knife-edged handle. I had to change arms every hundred yards. I would willingly have dumped the miserable thing at the side of the road, only Hugh very nobly took turn and turn about in carrying it. Whenever we asked a sentry how much further we had to go, the answer was always either 'three kilometres' or 'just round the next corner'. When we did eventually arrive, we must have marched at least eight miles. Ten days of short rations must have taken more out of us than we thought, as we were all pretty well 'done' when we arrived.

We were then searched. They took away my mug and a gin bottle I was using as a water bottle. They failed to find my six Egyptian pound notes, which I had not hidden at all carefully.

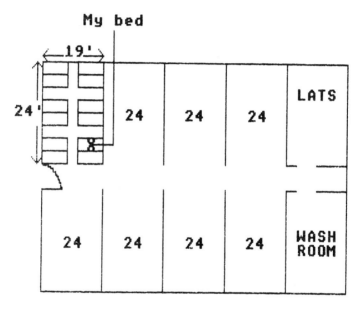

A Plan of the Hut at Bari

It was a bit congested; 24 feet by 19 feet, day and night accommodation for 24 officers. The beds—double decker of course—were brand-new, and the most comfortable wooden beds I met. The planks, being longitudinal and going the whole length of the bed, had a bit of give in them. The only snag was that if one sat on them with the mattress rolled back, one was apt to get one's behind nipped. My bed companion was John Bowley, and above us we had

Jock Holden and George Hooker. Our hut was only recently put up, because the older huts were very bug- and flea-ridden.

For exercise we had some road space and a scruffy area behind our hut; in addition, for the first half of our stay we had a two-acre olive orchard; this was subsequently filled with bivouac tents and used as a compound for ORs.

The greatest point in the camp's favour was its beautiful water supply. There were no actual taps in the wash rooms, but beautifully sweet and ice-cold water gushed forth all day and night. It was the first and last camp I was in in which there was no 'water problem'. The greatest black mark against the camp was the interminability of the roll calls and the miserable quality of the Italian officers. The average roll call lasted about 1¼ hours, and some as long as 4 hours; we had two every day and sometimes more.

The only books I managed to get hold of were the Bible and Boswell's 'Life of Johnson', Vol 2, and these only for very short periods.

I used to walk in the mornings with Crispin or someone and every evening Hugh and I used to walk for a couple of hours. New batches of prisoners kept arriving but they were kept segregated and one could only converse with them through a couple of barbed wire fences; we were nominally in quarantine. Among the new arrivals were Donald Mackenzie and a fourth member of the clan in the person of the young Earl.

The food, although a lot of people found it quite inadequate, I found to be sufficient. Some people got so hungry as to stoop to stealing food from their companions. My respect for colonels suffered a severe blow here and never recovered the whole time I was 'in the bag'. There were some bad types.

The food consisted almost entirely of fruit and vegetables—tomatoes, onions, olives, plums, peaches, figs, nuts and later on, apples and pears. Occasionally we had a hot rice or macaroni stew. The sudden change in diet, fortunately, did not have the same effect on my inside as it did on some of the people!

We played bridge occasionally and talked a lot. 'General interest' talks drew large audiences. One I remember by Padre Collins was on the Varsity Boat Race.

I recollect one afternoon which went particularly quickly; Bill Bowes came and sat on our bed, and most amusingly told us the story of his life. He then treated us to some devastating card tricks; he is a member of the 'Magic Circle' at home.

One evening, after the time we were confined to our bungalows, someone looking out of the window saw one of the ORs in the adjacent compound go towards the sentry on the gate between the two compounds. When he got within five yards of the sentry, without any warning the sentry shot him. One of our doctors went to the door of our hut and asked the sentry to allow him to attend the shot man. The sentry refused, and threatened the MO with his rifle. Meanwhile, we could hear the man groaning. Ten minutes later, an Italian officer came, and gave permission to attend the soldier. His condition was hopeless and he died before he reached the MI room. The next day our MO was asked by the Italians to sign a death certificate giving 'heart failure' as the cause of death.

Some of my other impressions, at random, are:

1. Tommy Sampson playing his cornet softly and sweetly in the bungalow.

2. Evening concerts on the boundary fence between our compound and the OR's. Apart from Sampson, there was little talent, but the Admiral and Bob Caterall had some amusing stories and songs of what we subsequently scornfully called 'transit camp taste'.

3. Crispin Ardern pacing round the orchard, clad only in a blanket à la kilt, held in position by a webbing belt.

4. Britz—a typical Boer giant—who was in the bed next mine. He was always 'agin the Government'. He told Crispin (room commander) that he refused to do things he was told to do, but didn't mind doing things that he was asked to do.

5. The first Red Cross parcel we got—one between ten—and how carefully we rationed it out.

6.People going about barefoot, to save boots and stockings.

7. Queueing for food.

So life went on for about a month; people then started to be moved to their permanent camps. The first lot to go were a group of about 60 Field Officers, including Robbie and Tony Law. Then all the South Africans below the rank of Major left. A week later 300 of our subalterns and captains departed, followed two days later by another 300 including Felix, Hugh, and John Bowley.

By now our bungalow was quite empty. We all slept in top bunks and converted the bottom ones into tables and forms where we could eat and play cards in reasonable comfort.

Food became more plentiful and the fruit better in quality. I found I had more than enough and was able to pass some over the wire to Sergeant Ryan, who had put up such a brave show in my little battle. I paired up with Crispin after John's departure. Roll-calls became comparatively quick and we even got a whole Canadian Red Cross parcel each. One pound of real butter. Whew!

On August 17th, about 120 of us, mostly Field Officers, were warned to be ready the following morning. We spent the evening hiding away the few takeable possessions we still had. I had only my pound notes to worry about. I hollowed out a cake of soap and put two inside it, and then washed with the soap to cover up traces. I squeezed two into the seams of my shorts and the others into the lid of my suitcase. John Holden had a prismatic compass for which he made a little sling and which he hung in a well-concealed portion of his anatomy, the only snag being that it made walking a painful process for him!

We got up at 4.30 the next morning and humped our possessions, paliasse and blankets to the gate, where we dumped our bedding. We were then searched. By 8 a.m. we were all ready and formed up for our march to the station. It transpired however that there had been a 'technical hitch' and our departure had to be delayed. We were put into a very small hut. At about 4 p.m. we were told, 'No move today'. Our bedding was reissued but there was not room on the floor for all the mattresses to be laid out, so we had a most uncomfortable night. The following day we were ready to move by 6 a.m. At 10 a.m. the 'no move today' order came again. We were furious. After pressure, they moved us to a larger hut where we could all just lie full length. To pacify us we were given a British Red Cross parcel between two, which had to be eaten by the next day. That was grand. Crispin and I had great fun taking alternate dips with my invaluable teaspoon into the condensed milk, jam, and all the other delicacies. We went to sleep really gorged! The next morning we actually did get under way. We were taken in lorries to the station and were very impressed by the distance we had marched on arrival.

Again, we had a very comfortable journey, this time five to a first class carriage. The route was mostly within sight of the sea, and the scenery was pleasant. We reached Chieti Scala at about 8 p.m. the following day. On the journey we bought papers pouring scorn on 'England's 10-hour invasion of Europe'—the Dieppe raid.

On detraining, we were told we had to march to the camp. They

said the distance was 500 metres. We groaned and prepared ourselves for a least a five mile march, but their estimate this time
proved accurate. We were soon within the gates, being searched by
the light of a searchlight. The two pound notes in the folds of my
shorts were unfortunately discovered; bowever I was given a receipt
for them. We were then put in Bungalow 4, pending a reshuffle the
next day.

11

Chieti, August 1942—September 1943

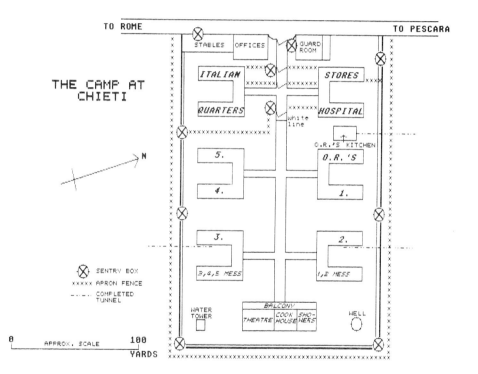

THE CAMP AT CHIETI

    The camp consisted of six U-shaped reddy-brown single sto-
reyed buildings, arranged symmetrically on either side of a tarmac
road. At the end of the road, on the side of the camp opposite the
gate, was the cookhouse block. The camp had been built in 1940 as
a civil internment camp, but had never been occupied. It was situated on the main road and railway from Pescara to Rome.

The camp was enclosed by a brick wall about 15 feet high, on top of which were built wooden sentry boxes. The town of Chieti stood on a hill some 800 feet high, to the south and overlooking the camp; it made a very fine medieval silhouette. To the north the ground was flat and our view restricted. On the north-east were the hills, separating us from the narrow coastal plain, which culminated in the hills on which Chieti stood. To the south were unfriendly, bleak mountain slopes. The best view was to the west, out over the main gate. The land was flat and well cultivated for about twelve miles, and then the Apennines loomed up and the whole view was dominated by the famous Gran Sasso, 14,000 feet high.

The South Africans who had left Bari about a fortnight before us had been the first inmates of the camp. The two batches of subalterns and captains had followed them, and so our arrival put the number of inmates to about 1,300. The arrival of our party, containing such a high proportion of Field Officers, was rather resented by the earlier arrivals. They had got the camp running very smoothly and there were committees organising such things as the Red Cross, Education, Messing, and Entertainments. They were naturally rather alarmed that a bevy of senior officers would tactlessly launch themselves into camp politics and possibly gum the works! I am glad to say that their fears proved groundless. Colonel Gray took over as Senior British Officer and a Lieutenant Colonel was put into each bungalow as bungalow commander, but the committees were left intact.

The day after our arrival the Field Officers were distributed amongst the five bungalows. I remained in Bungalow 4 and formed a clique with Crispin, Stanley, Scottie, Trot Taylor and Fane Harvey. We were put into Room C, with eight other majors. We had wooden stools, but otherwise our accommodation was no better than at Bari. I had a top bunk with Crispin Ardern underneath me. One great improvement on Bari was that we had dining halls sufficient for everyone to sit down at two sittings. We also had plates, forks, and spoons, but no knives or mugs. I got bored of trying to spread my bread with my teaspoon and so fashioned a miniature cricket bat out of box wood with a razorblade and some broken glass, to use as a spreader. I took days and infinite care in making it, and had hoped to bring it home as a memento.

Education got going full blast within a week. I, full of initial keenness, enrolled for agriculture, Arabic and Urdu. There were, of course, no text books or notebooks, no blackboards and no proper accommodation. Most of the classes assembled sitting on the kerb of a pavement or in the shade of a courtyard. Atty Brooks ran a most excellent course on agriculture which, besides crops and livestock, included botany, organic chemistry, zoology and estate management. Sydney Carver took the Arabic class, which proved to be a 'jolly', not very serious but enjoyed by all. Chris Ackroyd gave a brilliant series of lectures on Political Science and the British and American Constitutions. I remember him standing up, eyes half closed, gold teeth flashing in a half-smile, barefooted and clad in a blanket skirt and with another blanket worn as a toga. He was terrific and drew large audiences. Later, Trot Taylor, at my suggestion, gave a series of lectures on the development of tactics throughout the ages, and finally another series on the American Civil War. It was a brilliant effort, considering he had no reference books.

Basketball and tennis quoits got going. I found walking to be the best form of exercise and the most economical on one's most limited wardrobe. Stan and I went to a Scottish country dancing class on three afternoons a week. It was great fun, good exercise, and economical on clothes as we danced barefoot and wearing only shorts. Hugh, after recovering from German measles, also joined the class.

For a brief period, about 70 people a day were allowed out for a route-march, escorted by about 100 sentries. We used to go about 1½ miles up the road and then back again after a short rest. The walks were eventually stopped owing to our lack of footwear and respectable clothing.

Entertainments got going quickly. One-act plays and simple revues were put on in the 'tunnel room' (so called because our first attempt at a tunnel was discovered there by the Italians). Every Saturday evening there was an outdoor concert, with songs, community singing, accordion, piano, cornet, and banjo solos, together with some crude stories. It was at one of these that Richard Fletcher made his bow, singing 'Ave Maria' delightfully.

Cigarettes and matches were very scarce and it was a common sight to see senior officers picking up other people's fag ends. Someone almost forfeited his life by tieing a particularly juicy fag end on the end of a length of white cotton and jerking it away when some nicotine-starved officer stooped to pick it up. There is a story of how when Colonel Steele was having an interview with the Italian Commandant in his office, the Commandant threw the butt of his cheap cheroot out of the window, and was somewhat surprised when Steele instantly pursued it through the window!

Autumn came. The rain and cold, coupled with the almost complete lack of clothing, made life miserable. The arrival of our first letters kept us going. General interest lectures became popular, because by getting as many people as possible into one room one was able to keep reasonably warm for a period. I gave a lecture on the Egyptian Army, which went down reasonably well as I could always fall back on recounting amusing incidents if things started to drag.

In November the South Africans left, and we were able to thin out a bit. Crispin, Scottie, Trot, Fanny and I moved into Room F and had the luxury of a table. We were a happy party. We played a lot of bridge, and some light-hearted poker. I remember winning £30,000, his wife, and his house on Epsom Downs from Fanny one evening! By snatching it away from Scottie after lunch each afternoon when he fell asleep, I managed to read 'Gone with the Wind', which I enjoyed immensely. I was co-opted to teach a syndicate in the Staff Course, which we held in great secrecy. I also gave two lectures to the Gunner Discussion Group (Chairman—Friar Tuck!)

I was indeed lucky in having such congenial company to see me through those black days.

Water was very short, food scanty, clothing nil. My boots gave up the ghost in earnest. I was very proud of the repair I effected. It was carried out using a fly-swat as material, and a stone, a tin opener, and the inevitable tool for taking stones out of horses' hooves as implements. Thanks to a bit of looting when the South Africans left, I procured myself a wooden handle for a mug. The handle I still have, and it has become a prized memento. It has been attached to many tins, two of which were destroyed by American bombs!

I enjoyed the bartering that went on. If I managed to buy a slab of chocolate for two fewer cigarettes than a rival gave, it kept me happy for a week. Bacon, I remember, was worth 40 cigarettes at the time; I had a bargain with Stan whereby I gave him 30 cigarettes a week and each time he got bacon in his parcel, he gave it to me. As most parcels contained bacon, most weeks I had the exultation of having paid ten cigarettes fewer than anyone else! Peter Benson was an excellent bargainer and when he and I joined forces I appointed him as my sole agent with most gratifying results. Whilst on this delectable subject, I recall hearing a question asked which I do not suppose had ever been asked before in the history of man; it was, 'What is a fair price for a pair of shorts, in cheroots?'—but that was later on, when clothes were obtainable, at a price.

Fortunately one's sense of humour became sharpened. It was very amusing to see the various types of dress and undress the people appeared in for walking up and down the road from the cook house to the white line. I remember Stan, looking more ecclesiastical than ever with his shining bald head poked through a hole cut in the centre of a blanket and a leather belt perilously binding his midriff. Blanket kilts became popular, and shoes made from newspapers or cardboard boxes.

Lett, White-Abbot and Notley produced a weekly news commentary on Sunday mornings. These meetings were rightly very popular and attended by almost the whole camp. To start with they were held by the well, but subsequently in the theatre. There we stood happily for an hour, packed tighter than sardines, listening to what I called 'morale uplift'. Lett, especially, took immense trouble, and kept the camp optimistic in a most laudable way.

To our disgust, we had an upheaval just before Christmas. Crispin and Fanny, together with a number of other Field Officers, were whisked off at very short notice to a Senior Officers Camp. This caused a reshuffle of rooms on Boxing Day. We four were moved back to Room C, which we shared with Knight, Wall, Russell and Moss. We had single beds—folding iron ones with canvas bottoms. They were very comfortable after our wooden ones.

There was a bit of friction between the two cliques, and after about three weeks Knight and Co. moved out and Peter Benson and McGowan moved in. From then until we left in September were the most pleasant months of my captivity.

Red Cross clothing arrived in February. It was quite difficult to recognise people with everyone dressed in new battledress, boots, and overcoats. Our first next-of-kin parcels arrived in March. It was a wonderful thrill getting that first parcel—everything had that clean 'pre-bag' smell. I could well imagine myself to be in Clifton's or Boots! The messing improved; we handed our meats, fish and puddings into the mess, and it was served up communally, which was much better and more economical.

Peter, Mac, Scottie, Stan and I bought a set of mah jong for 40 tots of vino and 100 lire! We spent an incredible number of hours play-

NO.4 BUNGALOW, CHIETI

ing it. We also had great games of Totopoly.

By this time, there was terrific 'house spirit' in all the bungalows, just as in a public school! Basketball was the most popular game until April, Geoff Cornish leading our bungalow team to victory in the final. By April we had a fair sprinkling of Americans in the camp, and so softball became the rage. I enjoyed it tremendously. I was enrolled in a 'first division' team captained by Tim Toppin and including Smash Kilkelly, Bill Bowes (as pitcher), John Bowley, Red Davies and John Blackwell. Our chief rivals, until the All-Yankee team appeared were 'The Greens' who included Tom Meehan, Algy Collins, Jimmy Needler, Peter, and the rest were Green Howards. The Americans kept most complicated statistics and averages; Smash and I were highly surprised and honoured to find ourselves in the'Big Ten Batters' in the sports section of the Associated Press news sheet run by Larry Allen!

We never quite mastered the 'patter', nor did we ever get used to our Yankee coach's cries of encouragement, such as, 'C'maan gang', 'Give'm da woiks, fellers', 'That's pitchin' 'em, Bill, you've got'm swinging like a rusty gate', and so on. I won the nickname of

'The unsporting major' from my team mates. It happened this way. The first time we played the Yankees I had to race like blazes on one occasion to get to home base and, not having mastered the approved 'slide', I had to run straight into their 6 foot 3 inch catcher and knock him endwise; whereupon I was severely censured by the umpire who told me he would send me off 'next time'. It was all great fun!

Volley ball was also popular. We had quite a good room side, especially after Doc Simmons moved into our room. He was a tower of strength, being immensely tall! I quite often used to play games of baseball, volleyball and basketball all on the same day, a thing I could not do now (February 1945).

The theatre was the backbone of our camp structure. The acting was of a very high standard. Among the highlights were Geoffrey Lewis as Shylock, Alan Glover in 'The Man who came to Dinner', Paul Hardwick and John Metcalfe in all their parts, James MacFarlane in his female roles, and Bill Bowes as the half-witted hobo in 'Of Mice and Men'. The props department showed great powers of improvisation, especially in the early days of no clothes. Of the home-written plays, Jerry Chambers' 'The Aunt Isobel Affair' was the best. He had hoped to re-write it for publication at home, but unfortunately he was shot in escaping from the train.

In the world of music, Tony Baines and Tommy Sampson were the heroes. Baines ran the Symphony Orchestra, which unfortunately was a bit weak in the violin section, and Sampson the Dance Band. Sampson's band was excellent, especially after it was reinforced by two Yankees, both professionals, one a drummer and the other a trumpeter. Other smaller 'combinations' were run by Claude Godwin (accordion band), Pitts (teatime orchestra) and Foulsham (small dance band). A later acquisition was Perry, who had been music arranger for Walt Disney before the war. The amount of work put in by Tommy Sampson and the others was gigantic. All music had to be written from memory and the scores copied out by hand on any odd bits of paper that were available. Most of the experts played in at least three of the different bands or orchestras.

The library, with the arrival of private book parcels, became quite well stocked. The Italians eventually produced a cinema, which operated in one of the courtyards. There were some quite good films and some very bad ones. They were all in Italian. One film—I think it was 'Raffles'—started off with some very pleasant scenes of Canterbury Cricket Week; it was a terrific anticlimax when one of the Canterbury constables, when clearing the ground after the lunch interval said 'scusati' and 'prego'! They showed us a Laurel and Hardy film—Stanio and Olio they were called!

Later on, small parties were taken down to the local river, the Pescara, in the early mornings for a bathe in three feet of muddy water. This was very welcome; it was nice to get outside for a walk, and it gave one the chance of a much-needed wash. In the 13 months I was at Chieti I was only able to get four hot showers, so it was a matter of cold baths in hand basins.

Rollcalls, on the whole, were not much of a nuisance; in fact when they were held in our rooms we did not even bother to get up for them. The only 'incident' was due to a misunderstanding on the part of the Commandant, which resulted in a 'sit-down' strike by us and a four-hour rollcall; one officer was slightly bayoneted and one clubbed on the head with a rifle butt. On the whole, the Italians left us alone pretty well.

Our first Commandant was a funny, pompous little man who took a sneaking pride in all our activities: theatre, boxing tournaments, art exhibitions, and so on. Our second Commandant was a 'Blackshirt', very correct and distant. The nasty piece of work was the fascist interpreter, Crochet. He was tall with padded shoulders, a monocle, a black imperial, and he stank of scent. The best escape from Chieti was done by an Italian-speaking officer, 'W'. He did not let on that he knew Italian, and got the job of typing in the office. He worked there for two months, carefully watching every gesture and noting every accent of the detestable Crochet. Then one evening the theatre people disguised him as Crochet—smell and all—and he brazenly walked up to the gate, ticked off the sentry for not saluting smartly, hailed two Italian soldiers—Jock Holden and another, disguised—and told them to hurry up with his suitcases or he would miss his train to Rome. In this way the little procession got past all the sentries and out of the gate, and made for the open country. Unfortunately Crochet himself went out of the gate ten minutes later. The bewildered sentries explained the phenomenon to him and the alarm was sounded. They were brought back two days later. There were no successful escapes, but a lot of good work was done. Some of the completed tunnels were masterly pieces of work. The longest was 110 yards long and included lighting and air pumps. When we left, three tunnels were in working order.

Morale of course gradually soared with Tunisia, Sicily, and the fall of Mussolini. A carabinieri's comment was, 'Benito finito, God save the King'! When nothing startling happened after the change of government, some people who had not learnt the art of occupying their time started to go nervy or 'round the bend'; four had to be sent to mental homes. I believe they all regained their sanity eventually.

Mac left for a new camp in July, and we got Tom Meehan into our room in his place.

Softball, volleyball, mah jong, totopoly, sunbathing, walking, reading, theatres, music, cinema; thus the time passed until September 8th—Armistice! But before describing the ensuing heartbreaking muddle, here is Bill Bowes' description of a certain afternoon in August.

'The POW has few, if any, days on which he can look back with a feeling of real pleasure. The best efforts of the stage and screen are at the most only an hour or two of forgetfulness of the four walls, sentries, barbed wire and tommy guns of every day life. Yet we at Chieti had one such day of pleasure, real pleasure, which even in our future English moments we are likely to remember and the memory cherish.

'It was a cricket match! not an England v Australia affair but a real match! A match that took us back to the village green, a match which even "base bawling" Yanks honoured with unexpected quiet enjoyment and moments of genuine applause. There was sufficient cricketing talent exhibited for even a strict theorist to find pleasure. There was some excellent bowling which included a hat trick by Gardner and the spin of F.R. Brown. There was some good batting including a fine "backs to the wall" innings by Beaumont (Yorks II) and a most academic display by Bull (Leicestershire). But of all the things that gave pleasure, it was the efforts of those "behind the scenes". That our POW cage could ever be made a cricket ground sounds impossible. The space available consisted of a barren rectangular piece of ground, covered with small stones, intersected by roads and gutters, and bounded by a cookhouse and many bungalows. A portion of the central road was distempered green. The theatrical props department had made a huge imitation roller and a large pavilion clock. The former held a place of honour near the sight screen (bed linen) and the latter, like all pavilion clocks, was "lord over all" on top of one of the bungalows, converted to dressing rooms and by a clever arrangement of stools and forms made a Members' Enclosure too. There was another imposing edifice, made of tables and blankets, which proved later to be a bandstand. Pitso's orchestra played light classical music for half the time, and Tommy Sampson's dance band was converted into a military band and played for the rest of the match.

'At 1.40 p.m. the groundsmen—Messrs Long and Short—began to roll the wicket. At 1.50 they marked out the creases and erected the wickets, specially made on wooden stands to go on the tarmac. The captains tossed. At 1.55 the umpires, in white coats borrowed from the Italian doctor's surgery, took the field, put on the bails and surveyed the crowd of spectators. Everyone in the camp had turned out and I have seen fewer spectators at County games. F.R. Brown (Surrey and England) led out the fielding side, and it was noticed that the wicket keeper had on a good pair of home-made pads while a pair of motoring gloves, specially padded, made excellent gauntlets.

'I need not dwell on the anxiety of the sports storeman who, with only half a dozen balls in stock, saw one after the other hit far away into "liberty"! I need not eulogise the cookhouse staff who served tea round the ground. I need not mention the comments hurled at an Italian officer who, knowing nothing of cricket, dared to walk across the ground. I need not tell you how excellent the cricket and the musical fare. What was marvelled at most was the excellence of the finish; it was very close indeed, a fight against time. Need I tell you why? A man inside the clock had been cleverly arranging things all the afternoon!

'Surely not a day in captivity—but a real August day in England.'

All I have to add to Bill's account is that I had to go in to bat to save him doing the hat trick! and as Freddie Brown was the other bowler I was quite satisfied in breaking my duck! Freddie on a tarmac road I found more devastating than on matting in Egypt in 1939.

So, all in all, Chieti was a friendly cheerful camp. We were all the same vintage prisoners and all shared the same hardships and handicaps. Spending so much time out of doors one got to know most people by name. The games, the theatre, outdoor evening concerts and the good weather combined with the very excellent communal spirit, triumphed over its disadvantages—congestion, lack of water, lack of clothes, lack of furniture and so on. It was the happiest camp I was in, though the most uncomfortable of the permanent camps.

12

Italy to Germany

On September 8th we were playing bridge in our room after supper when suddenly terrific cheering broke out. We did not need to ask what had happened. Singing and cheering lasted a long time. Eventually we got to bed, but I do not think any of us slept much as we were too excited. Rumour had it that British Staff Officers were in Rome. The next day the cook house produced a splendid 'liberty dinner'; it was a grand meal and we had most satisfactory indigestion after it!

I feel too strongly on the subject to discuss the rights and wrongs of the SBO's decision to keep the camp together and in situ. 'Keep cool, calm and collected' was his parrot cry, which was changed by many to 'cool, calm and be collected'! About four days after the armistice, Keslring's speech came over Rome Radio. The vast majority of our brave Italian guards that night climbed out over the walls and were not seen again. Civilians on the surrounding hills gestured imploring us to get away and take to the hills while the going was good. The SBO still clung to his policy and we had to post our own sentries to keep our own people in. One officer caught scaling the wall was put under close arrest. It was all tragic.

On the night of the 20th, German parachute troops surrounded the camp and officially took us over from the Italians. You can imagine the feelings of the camp, especially against the SBO.

The move away from Chieti started on the 21st. The move was by road. Peter and Tom were in the first batch to go. Two more batches left the next day and we were finally moved on the 24th. We went by road along the narrow valley through Popli to Sulmona. The camp was a big Other Ranks camp. All the Chieti people were still there. We were extremely lucky and were housed in the Officers' compound. There was an officers mess with mess waiters, white table cloths; in fact quite civilised. I shared a room for two with Trot Taylor. We had extremely comfortable spring beds with real mattresses, cupboard, chairs, and all the other luxuries we had forgotten about. The previous occupant had left behind his gramophone and records. In the evenings, Jimmy, Peter and Tom used to come for a concert, some comfort, and a game of bridge or cribbage.

We made an unsuccessful attempt at getting through the wire one night. Then we decided that our only chance was to await an oportunity to slip away on the journey.

We spent six days of glorious weather in the greatest luxury we had encountered. Walking, sunbathing, reading, and interminable discussions on what might have been 'if only . . .' and conjecture as to what was to happen to us. Some people firmly believed that the Germans would find it impossible to transport us out of the country. The super-optimists thought we were being collected in an area where there was not likely to be much fighting and where we would eventually be relieved by our own forces; the super pessimists had visions of massed executions!

The mountains rose very steeply to the south. Halfway up one vertical face was a 12th century hermitage built on a very narrow ledge. The outside wall of the house was a prolongation of the vertical cliff below. We heard later that the Germans before they evacuated the area had turned 36 88mm. guns on to the building and completely destroyed it as they suspected POWs were sheltering there.

In the camp, besides ourselves and the ORs were a good many elderly Jugoslav officers, typical bandits.

At midday on the 30th we were ordered to fall in with our kit. We were issued with a Red Cross parcel each and German rations for three days. They started moving us by lorry to the station at 2 p.m. We were the last to go, and did not leave till after dark at 10 p.m. Just before we left, two officers were brought back, both shot while trying to escape from the station. One was killed, the other badly wounded. The Field Officers were put in 2nd class carriages; everyone else was in cattle trucks. I unfortunately got separated from Trot and the others. As it was pitch dark when we arrived I was not able to see exactly how many guards we had or where they were. We moved out of the station at about 11 p.m. We were very weary after having stood in the sun all afternoon and evening. We had several stops and I made up my mind to try to get out of the window at the next stop. The sentries (we seemed to have about six in our coach, mostly in the corridor) dismounted when the train stopped, but it was so dark that I would have had a very good chance of getting clean away. I changed seats so that I got next to a window. At the next stop I grabbed my Red Cross parcel, pulled down the window, and just as I put my leg out there was a rattle of tommy gun fire. I withdrew my leg and decided to wait for a later stop. The train then went much faster and did not stop; I fell into a heavy sleep. It was daylight when I woke up. I was furious with myself, especially when I heard that forty people, including Peter Benson, had managed to escape. I found Trot; he had done exactly what I had done; in fact the tommy gun fire had been directed at him. We decided that we would go together the next night.

The people in the cattle trucks had been lucky. There were no guards in the trucks with them, but the doors were locked and the windows wired. One truck had been left unlocked, and all the occupants had got away. Others had cut their way through the windows.

We got to Rome before midday. We waited about two hours at a junction on the north edge of the city, and then began our long journey northwards. We passed aerodromes and railway coachyards which proved by their chaos the extreme accuracy of the American bombing. We made very slow progress until just before dusk when the train got a new lease of life and went infuriatingly fast. It stopped only twice that night, and both times at floodlit stations where escape was impossible. We sat up all night, but in vain. No-one escaped that night.

The next day we crossed the Po. We talked to Van Sickle who knew the Brenner area very well, and he suggested we should try to get off at Bolsano and make for the Murano valley, 75 kilometres up, which was the Swiss frontier. He drew us a sketchmap of the area. Our luck now turned. We saw that the sentries stood on the running boards at a halt, and stayed there until the train had gathered speed, when they trooped back to their carriages; there was approximately half a minute when the non-corridor side of the train was unwatched. Unfortunately, this side of the train was on the inside, so we would have to jump on to the permanent way. The moon did not rise till about midnight. It was pitch dark as we were nearing Bolsano. I prepared my haversack and my untouched Red Cross parcel, put on my greatcoat and gloves, and bandaged my hands with puttees. The train stopped in an ideal place; the sentries dismounted. Eventually we moved off again. The guards remained on the running board for what seemed an interminable time, and the train gathered speed quickly. At last the moment arrived. Trot climbed out of the window and jumped off; his kit was thrown after him. I put my legs out. The train seemed to be going very fast—25 m.p.h., I was told afterwards—I sat on top of the window, jerked myself off, and turned in the air to face the engine. I seemed to spend an awfully long time in the air and it crossed my mind that I might have jumped down a precipice. However, I landed squarely on both feet and was bowled violently over on to my face, fortunately missing the rails and all other obstructions. I picked myself up and bounded into the ditch, and enjoyed the wonderful sight of the red tail lamp of the train getting further and further away. I unwound my puttee bandages and felt myself for injuries. My face was bleeding pretty freely and my left knee was bleeding; otherwise all was well. I walked back down the line to find Trot. I had gone about 20 yards when I found myself on a steel girder bridge; I thanked my lucky stars that I had not jumped a second earlier. I found Trot in the ditch about a hundred yards back. He reported a painful ankle and a nasty cut on the back of his head. We walked along the line picking up our belongings which had been thrown out after us. The train must have stopped a mile or two further on because we heard a fusilade of shots which was always their habit at any halts.

We climbed down off the railway embankment and found ourselves on a footpath running alongside the railway. We followed this for half a mile, when we crossed to the west side of the railway. The moon was up by now and we could see the mountains. We walked due west until we came to the river, and walked along the tow path. We were scarcely able to resist singing, we were so pleased with ourselves. After a mile or two, Trot's ankle got very painful and my knee stiffened up. We recognised the valley we were aiming for; our problem was how to cross the wide, fast flowing river. After a while, a large concrete bridge loomed up ahead of us. We crept up to it. Apparently it was not guarded, so we decided to walk boldly across it. The bridge had been built to take a by-pass road which was under construction. We got across safely, and were just blessing Dame Fortune when we saw ahead of us a watchman guarding some road building machinery. He flashed a torch on to us. We must have looked a curious limping pair. We expected a challenge at any moment, but we walked on unconcernedly, and all was providentially well.

We now cut across country towards the hills to the north of the valley. It was very difficult going. Getting through vineyards in the dark is very hard work, especially when it is agony to bend your knee. We picked and ate beautiful apples and grapes all cold and wet with dew; they were marvellous. Progress was slow, so when we met the main road up the valley we decided to walk along it. We walked about 5 miles, and twice we had to cower in the ditch when a bicyclist and a car passed. Now however Trot's ankle seized up; it was obviously sprained. We had no hope of making the mountains. I left Trot by the side of the road and went in search of a hiding place. I found a place in an apple- cum vine-orchard. We ate more apples and grapes, lay on the ground and were soon asleep. I woke first; it was 6.30 and the sun was up. We moved to a slightly better hiding place. Trot's ankle was in poor shape and I massaged it while he read aloud from the Rubaiyat. We ate some more apples and grapes. We planned to lie up till dusk and then, if Trot's ankle permitted, to move further up the valley when it got dark.

By an amazing bit of bad luck, the farmer chose this day of all days to harvest his apple crop. The pickers arrived at about 8 a.m. Some of them started working on trees within ten yards of us. We were partially concealed behind a screen of vines. By noon we were still undiscovered. The womenfolk arrived with the harvesters' lunches. The men knocked off work, and one man and a woman selected a bank not more than three yards from us as a good spot for their lunch. The woman eventually spotted us and with a shriek ran away. The man however came over to us and we told him what we were. They were Austrians and had been conversing in German all morning. Reassured, the woman came back. They were very kind. They offered to get us civilian clothes, an offer we thought it best to decline. The Frau brought a basin of water and a mirror and washed my face and Trot's head for us. No wonder she had shrieked on first seeing us as my face was covered with dried blood!

We gave them a packet of tea and some soap, and they promised to bring us a map. Just as they were leaving us, a small boy, aged about 12, came into the orchard with a bicycle and saw them talking to us. The man went over and talked to the boy, who eventually went away. When he returned to us the man's attitude had altered. He showed us a better hiding place a little way away and left us. We opened up our parcels and had a good lunch. I went off into a doze after lunch; Trot woke me with a nudge. I looked round and saw that we were surrounded by German soldiers with tommy guns. They searched us and marched us off. We hobbled painfully about a mile back towards Bolsano, and were taken to a flak position. We were treated extremely well. A medical orderly dressed our wounds. Coffee and shaving water were produced for us, and more apples. The miserable little boy who had given us away was there, I suppose claiming the reward then being offered for escaping prisoners.

A very smart young sergeant was detailed as our escort. His mother was a Scot and his father had been in the Embassies in London and Washington. He spoke English well, and admitted frankly that he was fighting on the wrong side. His orders were to march us to Bolsano, but he managed to get us a lift, thank God, as it was over six miles away. We were conducted to various HQs, and no-one seemed awfully interested in us, perhaps because it was Sunday afternoon! It was a nice old-world grey town with some fine old buildings. Passers-by were friendly, and we had a number of cigarettes offered to us. Our escort apologised for not being able to take us into a cafe. The whole area was bristling with men in civilian clothes who carried rifles and wore armbands with the initials SOD on them. They were the local Austrian Home Guard. Eventually we were handed over to a Carabinieri Barracks, taken over by the Germans, next door to the railway station. We were put in a most insanitary cell which contained two iron beds and nothing else. The windows, which looked out onto a courtyard, were wired and barred, and the door was padlocked and bolted. In the adjoining cell were four Germans, condemned to death for desertion. We were let out three times a day to go to the lavatory. Fortunately we were allowed to keep our food parcels, so we fed well. The only rations we were given were a cold cup of ersatz coffee and some millet soup. We spent a reasonably comfortable night, despite the unpleasant smell left behind by the previous inhabitants. We were not unduly depressed because, I think, both of us realised that the odds against our jaunt had been very much against us.

An air raid warning went about noon the next day. The condemned Germans were removed to the shelters, but we were left in our cell. The planes arrived twenty minutes later. A sound like that of an express train heralded the arrival of the first bombs. We threw ourselves onto the ground. The explosions shook the cell so much that part of the ceiling came down and a bit of the inner wall fell on the calf of my sound leg. We crawled under the iron beds. The next wave dropped their bombs even closer and we gave up hope. The cell door, with its lintel, door posts, bolts, padlock and all was blown clean into the cell, bringing half the wall down with it. Bits of the ceiling rattled on the beds above us. We picked ourselves up, covered with dust and filth, and relieved our emotions with hysterical laughter. We hobbled out into the courtyard. No-one was about; presumably everyone was still underground. However, the gate onto the road was locked, and we were in no condition to climb over it and make a getaway. We sat down behind a buttress and had the pleasure of seeing the horror-struck look on the face of our warder when he saw the state of our cell and the absence of his charges.

Our cell was swept out and a sentry was substituted for the door. Half an hour later, to our surprise, Major Ferguson of the US Air Corps, who had been with us at Chieti, was ushered into the cell. 'Say, can't a fellow even go to a down-town gaol house without meeting you fellows' was his greeting. We got back at him with severe censure on the way his colleagues had made our cell so draughty! He, it turned out, had jumped out of a train the previous night, had been caught and brought in by road. He said the train he had jumped off was in the station now. We were very worried as to their safety. Later in the evening five British ORs were put into our cell, which made it rather crowded. They had escaped from the train during the air raid. The train had apparently been just the other side of the station. The guards had left the train with all the prisoners locked into their trucks. Fortunately, on the journey up, one truck load had managed to cut a hole in the floor of their truck large enough for a thin man to squeeze through. Someone had got out and released all the other trucks. The train was not hit, but it must have been a nasty experience.

We had a most uncomfortable night. There were warnings during the night, but to our relief nothing happened. At midday the next day we were marched to the train. We saw the results of the bombing. It had been uncannily accurate. The station was a shambles, with rolling stock thrown all over the place. The main road bridge had been hit and partially destroyed. We had been incredibly lucky as the buildings on either side of us were flat. A warning went as we got into the train. We did not move out for half an hour. We breathed a great sigh of relief as we drew out of the station; the

AckAck had just opened up.

We had the luxury of a first class carriage. The German officer told us that if anyone jumped off the train, the guards would shoot ten of his comrades! I thoroughly enjoyed the comfort of the train and the wonderful scenery of the Brenner Pass. The kit of two officers who had escaped was produced for us and we took what we wanted from it.

We reached Moosburg at first light the next day. We only had short way to walk to the camp.

13

Moosburg October 6th—December 8th 1943

Stalag VIIA was a big French Stalag cum transit camp for all ranks and nationalities. It was divided into compounds. The French were allowed more or less free movement within the camp, but we, the Jugoslavs, Russians and Italians (!) were confined to our compounds. Our train load was put into a compound containing three huts, one for officers and two for ORs. Rawlinson had been senior officer on the train, but apparently had been a bit weak, because little Padre Chutter organised a coup d'état and installed me as 'Compound Commander'. Rawly took it very well and we became good friends. I very much enjoyed having a certain amount of responsibility for the first time for almost eighteen months. The accommodation was awful, in dark huts with three-storey beds in blocks of twelve. There were about 200 people in each hut, with one tap between us. The lavatories were disgusting and were outside the huts.

We were lucky as in our hut were two French sergeants who were permanently employed as sort of quartermasters. They were invaluable to us and got us on the 'black market' and the corruption of sentries right away. Our first evening there, six of us dined off roast duck! beautifully hot with gravy and sauce, obtained through the black market and cooked by our obliging Frenchmen, all for a packet of tea and a few cigarettes. I bought sixteen eggs for a tin of Nescafé, which I had boiled for my breakfast each morning. David Wolfers managed to get in a barrel of beer, which was very nice; I regretted it afterwards as it caused me to go outside in the cold too frequently during the night. On three occasions our Frenchmen took Jim Chutter, Trot, and myself to the French theatre, once for a concert and twice for plays, one of which was by Ben Jonson— translated into French of course. We had Tommy Sampson and the American bandsmen in our party, and were able to return hospitality in a small way.

The Americans left after a few days and a few dribs and drabs came in, but we were able to thin out and make ourselves more comfortable. Our sentries were bribable with cigarettes. I had to go to hospital each morning as my face and knee were still bound up. I managed once or twice to buy my way into the compound where my original trainload were in residence. Scotty had very kindly salvaged some of my kit for me, including my precious rug, the mah jong set, and the beautiful sponge Peter had presented to me. I later got back other bits of my kit which had been looted by other people.

The weather was quite nice and all told our first fortnight was quite enjoyable. We were very sorry when we received orders to move into the big compound where the rest of our Chieti people were, and which was already overcrowded. On my first day there I had a long stroll with Jimmy Needler; these became a daily feature and set the foundations of the most valued friendship I made. Like Heraclitus and his boy friend,

'   . . . I remembered
how often you and I
had tired the sun with talking
and sent him down the sky.'

The afternoons we spent reading or playing mah jong and the evenings normally playing bridge.

It was here that cooking first raised its ugly head. I shared with Trot; we were not a very good combination, as he was always wanting to brew up tea for which I could get up no enthusiasm, and so did not really pull my weight. One afternoon when I was entrusted with the cooking it started to rain, and I could not get the fire going. After half an hour's hopeless struggle I accidently set fire to my pillow, which burnt well. This was too much for me, so I returned to the hut with my tail between my legs and swore that 'I'd soldier no more'! People here designed and made most elaborate and efficient 'blowers' of the 'wind the handle' type.

I had a most pleasant morning by attending the funeral of a Gunner Officer. We marched to the cemetery along country lanes thickly carpeted with brown autumn leaves, and for the first time for six years I got that wonderful autumn smell. The country was very like our own water meadows, only the rivers were broader. The actual cemetery might have been within a quarter of a mile of

Kingsmere. I was surprised and grieved to see there the grave of Biddulph, who had been at The Shop with me, and had died here in 1942. We walked back through the town, which was very nice. There and back we must have covered a good eight miles.

Later on we had about four semi-parole walks. We were allowed to straggle within reason, and it was all thoroughly enjoyable. We stayed out anything between one and four hours. Another feature was the occasional hot shower we got.

On two occasions the YMCA provided us with excellent English films which were shown in the French theatre. One was a Fred Astaire and Ginger Rogers film, the other starred Katherine Hepburn and Cary Grant. These treats did a lot to make up for the disgusting living conditions. There were 200 officers in one dark insanitary hut, with no washing facilities, insanitary lavatories, three-decker beds and insufficient table space. All meals had to be two relays.

We had one very thorough search by the Gestapo. We were told we were moving to another camp and so we packed up everything we had, fell in and prepared to hump our kit to the station. However, instead of the station our destination proved to be another compound. Each of us in turn was searched. I was one of the first and was done while the searchers were still keen. I was rather proud of getting my pound notes safely through. I had them in my hand. They searched my overcoat, which I was wearing, then told me to take it off; as I did so I left the notes in my sleeve. The striptease went on until I was in my birthday suit. They were at last satisfied and I was allowed to dress again, retrieved the notes, and all was well!

After the search we were conducted back to different huts, but the same type. Our new compound was smaller than the old one which in all conscience had not been exactly spacious. Fleas and bed bugs flourished, but fortunately for some unknown reason I had a tin of Keatings powder in my escape haversack.

We were of course all longing to be moved to a permanent 'Oflag'. Looking back on Moosburg I remember the bad points—overcrowding, filth, bad food (fortunately we had a regular supply of American Red Cross parcels), darkness (it was often too dark indoors to read at midday), and the constant air of disillusionment and impatience. But besides these I remember my daily walks and talks, the lovely smells and scenery we encountered when we were allowed out, and the Nescafé from the American food parcels.

It was not until December 8th that we eventually left. The first snow of the year was falling. The Field Officers were put into 3rd class wooden-seated carriages, everyone else into cattle trucks. There were five of us plus one sentry in our carriage. Padre Chutter was in my carriage. He was very good value as he had a fund of very good stories. The seats were awfully hard and uncomfortable but we did have the great advantage of being able to see the countryside through which we passed. We crossed the Danube, which looked anything but blue! The scenery was very dull, flat and hedgeless. The pine and fir forests looked nice in their first coat of snow. We left about midday and arrived at Marisch Trubau at 9 p.m. two days later—a 57 hour journey. We were issued with bread and German bully each day, and each evening a Red Cross stall at some station we stopped at gave us a very excellent millet stew. I slept both nights in the luggage rack. It was very narrow and uncomfortable but better than sitting up on our wooden seats. I had just settled myself precariously in the rack for my third night when we were told that we had reached our destination.

We had about a mile and a half to march. We went through the deserted cobbled streets of the sleepy old town. We could not see much as it was pretty dark. On arrival at the camp, we had a very mild search, were quickly issued with bedding, and were shown to rooms.

Marisch Trubau

Our camp was the Czech Military College, and was situated on the edge of Sudetenland. It was by far the best equipped of the camps I knew.

The accommodation consisted of a big ugly four-storey building, new and centrally heated. The average size room was for twelve people, but there were big rooms complete with blackboards, and small rooms for two people. In addition there were some nice-looking chalet bungalows, mostly single-storey, but two double-storey ones. There was a good cookhouse, and dining halls (which we never used as such owing to shortages of furniture and crockery), a swimming bath, a football ground and a theatre. There was plenty of space for walking, both round the buildings and round the sports ground. The barbed wire was not conspicuous. Beyond the sports ground was a road with some nice-looking houses on the other side of it. The road seemed to be the popular walk on Sunday mornings for the well turned-out inhabitants of Trubau.

We spent a few days, rather crowded, in the 'biscuit factory' before the outside bungalows were opened up for Field Officers.

I was exceedingly lucky and got what I considered to be the best room in the whole camp. It was on the first floor of the 'chalet' that overlooked a small lawn and the swimming bath, and was quite close to the biscuit factory. My three room mates were not however ones that I would have chosen. Leatherdale was an elderly Indian army major, a silly little man who talked a tremendous amount, chiefly about Burma! He was unhygenic, most annoying, and too easy to bully. Johnstone was a very hot-tempered, red headed Scot, a Roman Catholic, and Rawlinson was a nice but very dull and long-suffering chap.

(This is where my prisoner of war diary ends)

Brunswick, December 1943—April 1945

When we arrived at Marisch Trubau we had of course been without letters from home for about five months. Jimmy Needler was one of the last people in the camp to receive a letter. When he got one from his wife he broke down. He came rushing to me and showed me the letter. It started, 'My stump is far less painful this week' and then went on to trivialities. Poor Jimmy, it was not for several months that he heard what had happened. His wife had been hit by a car in the black-out in Pudsey, and had had one leg amputated.

We only stayed at Marisch for about four months. It was the most civilised of the camps I was in. We pooled all our Red Cross food parcels and as a result we fed well. I spent most of my time reading, and once a week went to our theatre, and never ceased to wonder at the ingenuity displayed by putting on such well staged and well acted plays every week. But I must admit that prisoner of war life was really getting me down. It was about this time that I had a letter from Joane saying that she had got engaged to an officer in her mixed Anti Aircraft Regiment.

We then had a two day train ride to Brunswick. We were all put in handcuffs before being put into cattle trucks, twenty officer prisoners and two sentries locked into each truck. I foolishly had not put on my greatcoat by the time I was handcuffed. It soon got very cold and I asked the sentry to release me from the cuffs while I put on my coat. He refused. When it got dark, a friend of mine managed to unlock my cuffs and I put on my greatcoat and had a reasonably comfortable night, and put the cuffs on before it got light. I then had the pleasure of watching the sentry trying to work out how I could have put on my coat with my arms still handcuffed. He was miming the actions and shaking his head. We all burst out laughing. Another truckload was more enterprising. They all took their cuffs off and put them into the large bucket which acted as the lavatory. In the middle of the night they asked the sentry to empty the bucket as it was full. This he did. When dawn broke, he was horrified to find that none of the prisoners were manacled. Eventually an officer came and demanded, 'Where are your handcuffs?' Somebody answered, 'We don't know, the sentry threw them out of the door.' The officer left, muttering that the senior prisoner would be shot at the next halt!

Our prison (Oflag) was outside Brunswick and within a quarter of a mile of what we discovered to be a V2 flying bomb factory. Our 'cloak and dagger' experts managed to get this information back to the War Office by a coded message in a letter to an innocent addressee. This was in June 1944 and on August 24th American Flying Fortresses made a huge raid on Brunswick. I was with a group of friends outside our block, watching each successive wave of bombers dropping their bombs where the smoke markers showed them. Suddenly a marker came down much too close for comfort, so I and most of the others hurried to the cellar. A whole load of heavy bombs landed on our barracks and with them came the very latest anti-personnel bombs. Five of the group which I had been with were killed, including 'Smash' Kilkenny of the 8th Hussars who was a very good friend of mine. In the barracks there were about six large barrack blocks, four full of prisoners, one for the German Other Rank quarters, and one for administrative offices. Of these the German block was destroyed and the Administrative block was damaged. None of the prisoners' blocks were hit! but the anti-personnel bombs which resembled thick coiled springs caused a number of casualties.

It was in this camp that an organisation was set up to finance an Oflag VIII Fund for Boys Clubs at home. We all promised sizeable contributions from our untouched Army pay. The Duke of Edinburgh after the war made our effort the centre piece for his appeal to the nation for finance for boys' clubs. I was roped in to go on to the stage of a large crowded cinema in Uxbridge, soon after getting home, to appeal for funds. It was a huge success.

Our time at Brunswick was most exciting, especially at the time of the Normandy landings which of course we heard all about on our hidden radios. Ever since we were in Chieti, we had had at least one receiver working. The first one was more or less home made, from parts bought by a blackmailed or bribed sentry. All through these three years we heard every word of Churchill's wonderful speeches and, my goodness, how they boosted our morale.

In my prisoner of war diary I was not able to mention anything that might prove helpful to our enemies. But now, over forty years later, I think I should mention some points of interest.

Tunnelling was of course a main occupation in every camp I was in. I tried my hand at it, but I must admit I was useless at it; I could not stand the claustrophobia and knowing that every foot of tunnel you dug meant another foot of painful wriggling backwards you had to do when your stint was over. Soon I confined myself to watching out for inquisitive 'ferrets'. Efficient escape committees were formed, and forgers of documents, makers of escape clothing and map makers worked hard and unbelievably efficiently.

When we were in Brunswick a message was received from the War Office that they needed urgently the identity papers of a certain senior rank Gestapo man. We somehow also had warning of a large scale Gestapo search of our camp. So the Escape Committee asked for any prisoner who had experience in picking pockets to report to them. Out of a camp of just over 2,000 officer prisoners, about seven offered their services. They were all interviewed and the one with the best credentials was selected and at the end of the search produced exactly what was wanted. I never heard whether it was ever delivered to the War Office!

For the last six weeks of our captivity we were very hungry. Allied bombing had played hell with rail and road traffic and there was not enough food to go round.

On April 12th 1945, after hearing sporadic gunfire for the past few days, a jeep from General Patton's Army arrived at the camp and accepted the surrender of the German staff. On the next day, a small number of 'experts' were allowed to go into Brunswick. The 'wine expert', a hotelier by calling, brought back several cases of Imperial Tokay which an anti-Nazi wine merchant had managed to keep hidden from the looters and had given to our expert to celebrate the end of his war. Very good it was, too.

A day or two later we were flown to a transit camp in Brussels, and on April 24th we landed at an aerodrome in Buckinghamshire. We were driven in coaches along such roads as at times during the last three years we thought we might never see again. The chestnut trees were flowering, as it seemed, to welcome us. We were taken to a large house in Chalfont St. Peter where we had baths, were deloused, issued with new uniforms and generally made much of. I rang up my father and mother; the latter told me that Joane had been in touch with her and that she had told them that she had broken off her engagement and hoped that I would get in touch with her!

I got home the next day. It was great. We had been given extra ration cards. Kingsmere was not short of food, as my father very wisely had been keeping chickens on our island ever since the first year of the war, and the garden grew enough vegetables for a whole regiment. I arrived home weighing 7 st. 4 lb., and by the time Dick returned home about ten days later, I was up to 9 stone.

Dick, I should mention, had been captured at Salerno, where he was a Fleet Bombardment Officer. He too had spent some time in Moosburg and was then taken to an Oflag in Southern Germany.

I wasted no time in getting in touch with Joane and we met each other by arrangement in the foyer of a West End hotel. We had not met for eight years. I went up and visited her at Lowestoft where she was a subaltern in a mixed Heavy AntiAircraft Regiment. She then came down to stay at Kingsmere. We became engaged during a walk on Arethusa and St. Catherine's Hill. Then we went down to stay at Tenby House. We were married on June 25th. Dick was my best man. The reception, a large affair, was at the Gatehouse Hotel and our health was proposed by Gwillm Lloyd George—later Lord Tenby. We spent the first night of our married life at Flemings Hotel near Gloucester Road and then went on to Great Fosters near Egham, a lovely hotel and within easy reach of Wentworth Golf Club. We then spent our time at Kingsmere and at Tenby House, getting back to the much-loved pre-war routine.

Our Wedding Day
25th June 1945

16

Early Married Life and the War Office 1945—1947

I was appointed as a GSO 2 to the Training Directorate at the War Office. The Directorate was housed in the Horse Guards and I shared a beautiful office on the first floor overlooking the arch and Whitehall. I shared it with Athol Rowe, an old friend of mine, who was responsible for Coast Defence Training as I was for AA Training. Also sharing the office was my GSO 3 who was an attractive ATS officer; her particular responsibility was Radar Training. Our boss, I was delighted to find, was Major General Ambrose Pratt who was responsible for Royal Artillery Training complete.

During the two years I was at the War Office, Joane and I had three different homes. Our very first one was a mews flat above the garage and stables of a very nice country house between Cowley and Iver. This was found for us by Margaret Raitt. We were very happy there. Joane started learning the rudiments of housekeeping and cooking and played a fair amount of golf. I worked six days a week, 9 a.m.—6 p.m. After about six months we moved to a typical suburban house in Ruislip, and finally we were lucky enough to be able to rent Calvert's Cross in the Quaker village of Jordans, which was within five minutes' walk of Seer Green station and of Beaconsfield golf course. By that time, Joane had established herself as a member of the Buckinghamshire County Ladies' Golf Team and had represented Wales.

We had bought an aged Morris Minor for about double its price when it was new in 1933. It was very unreliable, but on the whole did us fairly well. On one journey to Kingsmere we got a puncture and found that we had left our jack behind. I managed to flag down a Gunner lorry, and very obligingly the troops managed to hold up the car on three wheels while I and the driver changed the wheel!

Ambrose Pratt asked me to become Hon. Sec. of the RA Cricket Club and, with his help, to get the fixture list for 1946 back as near as possible to the pre-war standard. This we succeeded in doing. The highlights of the season were the centenary match, RA v I Zingari, a two day match at Woolwich, the first post-war Gunner—Sapper match at Aldershot, and RA v the Harlequins whose side consisted of most of that year's University eleven. I was very pleased to make about 60 not out in the first innings.

In 1945 I was, thanks to Ambrose, elected a member of both the IZ and the Free Foresters, and very quickly I was co-opted on to both clubs' selection committees as Army representative. I was briefed by Brigadier General Willie Clarke, who had been doing the job for many years. After telling me the minimum standard at the game an applicant should have reached before being put up for the Free Foresters, he said, 'For the IZ a candidate should be an even better cricketer and most importantly should be someone with whom you would be delighted if he asked to marry your daughter'!

The War Office work was interesting mainly because by the end of the war about two thirds of the Royal Regiment were in AntiAircraft units, mostly in AA Command, and the senior officers and instructors were mostly Territorial Army officers waiting to be demobbed. We had therefore to train quickly a large number of Regular Army instructors and assistant instructors with little or no experience of AntiAircraft gunnery, on Gunnery Staff Courses, often rather against their wishes, at least until they realised what good career chances the training would open up for them.

Ambrose, when he heard that I normally lunched at a Lyon's cafe, very kindly put me up for membership of the Army and Navy Club (The Rag) in St James' Square. Once proposed I was allowed to use its facilities before my election. I went there for lunch one day and sat at a table for one. I spent my time looking around at the portraits surrounding the beautiful dining room, and enjoyed being waited on by liveried and bemedalled waiters. I spoke to no-one and no-one spoke to me. The next day I lunched there again. This time, at a single table next to mine, was sitting a very aged, irascible and lame old gentleman (probably a retired General). Poor man, everything was going wrong for him; he was brought the wrong soup, his wine was 'corked', and finally he found a hair in his apple tart. He summoned the head waiter and gave him a vigorous dressing-down. I was secretly rather enjoying all this until suddenly he turned to me and said, 'This Club gets worse and worse every day, doesn't it?'

I was taken off guard and all I managed to say was, 'Yes sir, it was much better yesterday.'

My stupid reply was the last straw for the old man. He seized his stick and hobbled away muttering. I had to go to Ambrose's office later in the day and so I told him that I must have ruined my chances of ever becoming a member of the club. I told him all; he roared with laughter and told me he knew who the old man was and that he deserved all that he got. As I went out of the door, Ambrose said, 'Thanks for telling me that; I'll dine out on that story for months!'

After I had been in the War Office for a few weeks, my father rang me up and told me that Brigadier Stebbings had told him on the telephone that I had been awarded the Military Cross for my brief encounter with the German Mark 4s. It made a nice wedding present. When I saw the list I was delighted to see that Sergeant Ryan had been awarded the DCM.

Soon after VJ Day the Director Royal Artillery held a Major General's RA Training Conference at the School of Artillery at Larkhill. Almost all Gunner General Officers, from the CIGS (Lord Allenbrooke) downwards attended. General Pratt was Chairman of the Meeting and on the final day of the conference he took me with him. Somehow I was allowed to attend the final Guest Night. I was told afterwards that Major Generals, Brigadiers and Full Colonels entered the anteroom unnoticed, but when a mere major (me) came in, people were nudging each other and asking who he was. After dinner the usual Guest Night games were played, and finally two chargers were brought into the anteroom and were ridden over jumps consisting of mess sofas. The final scene was of a Lieutenant General, a Brigadier and a Colonel, all on the same horse, trying to jump an 'in and out' of sofas. This was a fine sight, but rather unsuccessful!

Joane and I normally played golf together on Sundays and we played for which of us should chose which cinema we would attend at Uxbridge the following Saturday. On the Saturday, Joane would meet me at the station, bringing with her cold sausages and biscuits which we would have as our supper while watching the film. After a year or so we had alternate Saturdays off. By then our petrol ration had been increased slightly and so we were able to play in various mixed open meetings, and spend the occasional weekend at Kingsmere.

At about this time the Gunner Training Branches came under the DRA and we moved to the main building across Whitehall and came under General Cam Nicholson, whom I knew fairly well through Gunner cricket. We were sad to bid farewell to General Pratt, but I still met him occasionally at the Club, which was a great meeting place of old friends.

I stayed at the War Office for two years. General Nicholson asked me where I would like to go when I returned to Regimental service, and I asked to go to the Field Regiment in Hong Kong.

We thoroughly enjoyed our time at Calverts Cross. The only snag to it from my point of view was that from Seer Green station, alternate trains went to Marylebone and to Paddington. This made it very awkward for the return journey. If I left work five minutes early I would try to catch the 6.20 from Paddington; occasionally I arrived just in time to see the train pulling out of the station, so then I had to go back to Marylebone on the Underground and hurry to catch the 6.35 from there. On one occasion I missed that too and had to return to Paddington!

The summer of 1946 was a beautiful one. I managed to organise myself some good cricket and even played for the first time ever in the RA Golfing Society meeting at Royal St. George's, Sandwich. The winter was a bittery cold one and our water main was frozen up some hundred yards short of Calverts Cross; we had to collect our water in jugs from the nearest unfrozen house and drag it home on a sledge. Fortunately our plumber was the captain of the Jordans cricket team and I had managed to play for the village in two Sunday matches. I must have acquitted myself reasonably well, because the plumber gave us top priority in getting our water system going again. We were very sorry to leave Calverts Cross, but I had had my fill of commuting to London for two years.

We spent my embarkation leave at Kingsmere. I was of course very sorry to have to leave Joane behind, but I was assured that she would get a passage out within three months.

17

Hong Kong 1947—1950

I duly embarked on SS *Georgic* at Liverpool in August 1947. We had a most comfortable voyage to Singapore. There were two other Gunner Majors on board and each of them had been more or less promised postings to 25th Field Regiment in Hong Kong, which was rather worrying, but I felt that the DRA would pull strings sufficiently hard for me to assure me of that most sought-after posting, but the final decision had to be made on our arrival at Singapore by the CRA Far East Forces.

Our first port of call was Gibraltar. Jock Murray and I went ashore together, walked around the town and went up in the lift to pay our respects to the apes on the Rock. We sailed at dawn and as I watched the coastline of southern Spain drift by, I remember thinking what a miserable arid and dull place it looked. I would never have believed then that I was destined to enjoy many holidays there twenty to thirty years later. I did not get ashore at Port Said or at Suez, but I enjoyed my first trip through the Suez Canal. We had a short stop at Colombo and then went on to Singapore. The three rivals were driven to the RA Mess and the next day were interviewed by the CRA. Jock Murray and I were told that we were to be posted to Hong Kong to take over Batteries of 25th Field Regiment. The third was to go to 26th Field Regiment in Singapore.

Jock, being the senior, was to go on an aircraft carrier, and I on HMS *Cockade*, its escorting destroyer. We sailed the next day. Despite changing course to avoid a typhoon, we got mixed up with the tail end of it which made life very unpleasant in the overcrowded destroyer. I had to bed down in the wardroom after all the ship's officers had gone to their cabins. Fortunately they all went to their cabins very early, not, I think, for my benefit, but for their own comfort. *Cockade* seemed frequently to stand up on its stern and receive a couple of whacks on its hull from mountainous waves before falling forwards. The screws coming out of the water made an awful row doing airshots, and then the whole procedure started again. Miraculously I was not sick; I was probably too scared for that. However the gales moderated quickly and I enjoyed the rest of our three day passage.

My CO was a Colonel Beattie. He told me to take over command of 93rd Field Battery, which had been non-operational for almost a year and had been acting solely in an administrative role, receiving all ranks from the other Batteries who were due for Python, i.e. for return to the UK for their demobilisation. As a consequence morale was rather low and some of the senior NCOs were discards from the other Batteries. My job was to bring it up to the operational standard of the other two Batteries as quickly as possible.

The evening after my arrival at Gun Club Hill Barracks the officers of my Battery invited me to join them in a dinner at the Parisian Grill on Hong Kong Island. The meal was a real shock to me. The menu was spread over six pages, my T-bone steak overlapped my oval shaped plate on both sides and to top it all, when one of the subalterns complained that his steak was cold, after consuming two thirds of it, he was brought another one! He must have eaten the equivalent of two months' meat ration in England for one course. Rationing in England had been at its most severe for the last year at home. No restaurant was allowed to charge more than five shillings for a meal; whale meat and offal were served by most of them. In fact, when I had been invited by my Uncle Harry to lunch at the Athenaeum club one day, we were rather late going into lunch as we had been drinking with the newly appointed Minister of War. When he heard that I had recently arrived at the War Office, he said that he was a 'New Boy' too and wanted to hear my first impressions. So by the time the waiter had come to take our order, to Uncle Harry's disgust he told us that the only item on the menu for the meat course left was boiled tripe. I never thought that my first taste of tripe and onions would be at the Athenaeum! However, to return to Hong Kong, we had a most magnificent meal, and I much enjoyed my first two crossings of the harbour in the Star Ferry. The carrier and HMS *Cockade* were still anchored there.

After a month or so I was able to get a really good Battery Sergeant Major and between us by the time Joane came out we had achieved our first aim, that of parity with the other Batteries. When Joane came we were temporarily given a married quarter on the

Island, which was rather inconvenient. Very soon afterwards however we moved to a ground floor flat at 4 Chatham Road, Kowloon, which was only five minutes walk from Gun Club Hill. It was there that we first met 'Toots' and Yvonne Williams. He was then a Captain in the DCLI seconded to the 2nd/10th Gurkhas. They and their children have been our very great friends ever since.

We formed a Regimental Saddle Club, the horses consisting of about five China ponies and two or three Australian thoroughbreds imported by the Hong Kong Race Club but subsequently found unsuitable for racing and presented to us. I started giving voluntary riding lessons to the subalterns and before long we instituted Sunday morning paper chases in the New Territories, which were very popular. By then I had taught Joane the rudiments of riding. On one of the paperchases she was riding our grey China pony, Christmas. During the run, the field bunched up to cross an awkward stream and gully. Joane waited for everyone else to cross and just before she—or rather Christmas—started to go down the bank, to my horror I saw a water buffalo go berserk and charge straight at Christmas with its head down. Christmas managed to sit down on her haunches and the animal's horns passed just over her backside, and just behind Joane's, who had somehow managed to stay in her saddle. It was terrifying. That night, back in her stables, Christmas died of a heart attack.

We financed our Saddle Club by hiring our ponies out to a Chinese film-making company who paid us film-star rates for them.

Colonel Lamont took over command of the Regiment after about six months. The regiment took over a Nissen hutted camp at Tai Lam, on the coast road of the New Territories. Each Battery went there in turn for about six weeks. My battery's turn came soon after we were allotted the property and history of 37th Battery Field Artillery which had been awarded three Victoria Crosses in the Battle of Le Cateau in 1914. Our six week period included the anniversary of the battle, so I organised a Le Cateau Night all ranks dinner and cabaret to which, in addition to our own CO, Adjutant and Quartermaster, a representative party from the Buffs, to which my Battery was affiliated for training, were invited. It was a huge success. Morale was sky high; in fact David Lamont asked me to cool it down after a time! From that day for the next two years 93 Battery were not beaten by any other Battery in any match or competition, from rifle shooting to football, including cross country running, boxing, and even golf. I was very proud of them all.

During this time the Chinese Civil War was gradually getting closer to Hong Kong's frontier in the New Territories. A whole division commanded by General Evans came out and absorbed our Brigade Group. Training started in earnest for a defensive battle should the Chinese fail to stop at the frontier. It was a most interesting period and it included many exercises, organising observation posts on some of the highest mountains overlooking the frontier. Eventually the whole Division was deployed in defensive positions and we occupied our gun positions. The two troops of my Battery were both deployed on Fan Ling's 'new' golf course. My Battery HQ was a commandeered weekend bungalow belonging to one of the large trading firms, and our regimental Officers Mess was a fine villa belonging to a Mr Moller, a big ship owner. The Civil War eventually passed by the Colony and 40th Division sent troops to Korea. The remainder stayed in the colony, doubling the size of the original garrison.

Both Joane and I loved our three years in Hong Kong. We had a most efficient Chinese woman as our 'amah' who did all our household chores including the cooking. We made many friends including Grace and Peter Smalley and their great friend Jack Linnaker. Grace became Michael's most generous godmother and is still a very dear friend of ours. We played a lot of golf at Fan Ling and at Deep Water Bay, tennis at the United Services Recreation Club which adjoined Gun Hill Club Barracks, and rode in the Sunday morning paper chase meets and the hunts which became a popular feature of the colony's social round. It was all great fun. Joane managed to become ladies golf champion of Hong Kong. I and one of my subalterns, George Newton, won the Army doubles at lawn tennis, and Yvonne Williams and I won the mixed doubles at the USRC tennis tournament. The success that gave me the most pleasure was, strangely enough, at football. I had not played since 1935, in Malta, but the combined Officer and Sergeants Messes of our Regiment were challenged to a match against the rest of the Regiment. I was being closely marked by a Lance Bombardier of my Battery who was a member of the regimental team. He, bless him, seemed to mistake my hesitancy when confronting him with the ball for super guile! Then once, I was put right through the defence and was dribbling towards goal wondering what the hell to do when the goal keeper came out to deal with me: should I shoot? or try to dribble past him? At that moment the ball bounced up for no apparent reason and it was simple to lob the ball gently over the advancing goalkeeper into the goal. This must have so much impressed my Battery Selection Committee that I was invited to play for my Battery eleven at outside right in the second round cup tie in the inter-Battery competition of 40 Div. RA. I gratefully accepted. From the kickoff in our next match the ball went almost straight back to our goal keeper who kicked a towering clearance straight towards me on the touchline. Sergeant Major Pollitt was a spectator just beside me. 'Try to keep it in, sir!' he shouted. I soon saw that unless I did something drastic it was bound to go over my head and out of play, so I realised that my reputation demanded me to head the ball. I watched the ball and managed to get both feet off the ground at the moment of impact, and was amazed to see it go to the feet of our centre forward some thirty yards from me! This I think established me in the Battery team.

We eventually got into the final against the Independent Mortar Battery, which soon afterwards distinguished itself in Korea in the battle in which the Gloucestershire Regiment did so well. We were expecting a very close match. In the pre-match briefing we were told that by far their best player was their centre-half. Our captain (a Glaswegian) confidently said he would look after him. In the first five minutes of the game the two of them went for the ball and the opposing centre-half took no further part in the game! Eventually we won 6-0. The Gunner playing at inside right was a magnificent player. All his passes to me made me run a little bit faster than I thought I was capable of doing, so I was enabled to 'beat' my markers straight away. I have given this match too much space, but I was so pleased that as Battery Commander I played, because as far as I know, no officer played in any of the other Battery elevens. Gunner Marsden, my inside forward, was bought out of the Army by Rotherham United, and I had the pleasure of seeing him play his first match for them at Nottingham Forest, and score his first goal for them.

Joane and I for one leave took an 'indulgence' passage on the latest P & O cargo ship on a three week round trip of Japan. We called at about six different ports, including one on the northernmost island—Hokkaido—which was then, in January, under about three feet of snow. At one of the ports we smuggled ashore two bottles of whisky, a forbidden import at that time. We took them to a china shop and after much bargaining, and 'Auntie' having to be called in to sample it and to pass it as the genuine article, we came out of the shop with a forty piece hand painted dinner service which we still use on best occasions.

Confidential reports before the war were always taken very lightheartedly; since the end of the war they had become most important annual events. I had been lucky enough since the war to have had a series of good reports and had got all the necessary recommendations for both Regimental and Staff promotions. Then seeming disaster occurred. General Evans's Divisional HQ was in the Ladies Club House at Fan Ling, which meant that he constantly had to drive through our lines, and his RASC driver occupied a tent in my Battery lines. A number of units suffered an undue number of casualties from malaria, so quite rightly rigid anti-mosquito rules were insisted upon; no-one should have sleeves rolled up nor should they wear shorts after sundown, and all ranks should sleep under mosquito nets. General Evans used to drive our Regimental HQ wild by ringing up our CO whenever he saw anyone breaking these rules. One night my Battery Captain, walking through the Battery lines in the dark on his way to dinner in the Mess, saw a tent with its flaps open, electric light switched on, and a soldier bare from the waist up lying on his bed with no mosquito net. He recognised him as the General's driver. He mentioned this in the Mess and Colonel Lamont told him that when he returned after dinner, to look to see if the General's driver was still so blatantly ignoring orders. If he was, he was to put him under open arrest. This the Captain did. In the morning I rang up the General's ADC and told him that the General's driver was under open arrest, told him the reason, and said that should he want to deal with the case quickly I would arrange for the necessary witnesses to report to him at his convenience. I heard no more about it, until David Lamont summoned me to his office and told me that the Divisional Commander had given me an adverse report which I had to initial. The General's comments were, 'I disagree with the recommendations of the CO and consider this officer unfit to get a command and that his staff jobs should be second grade ones at a large Headquarters.' I was stunned. I asked Lamont if he knew the reason for this; he said he did not and had done his best to dissuade the General. I then asked him if he had told the General that it was on his orders that my officer had put the driver under arrest. He admitted that he had not.

It was with this absurd and unfair disaster hanging over me that eventually we embarked on the *Empire Fowey* at the end of my tour; a sad finish to a most successful and enjoyable three years. But I took away with me a silver salver inscribed, 'To Major A.E.G. Haig MC RA from the officers and men of 93 Field Battery RA July 1950'. I was assured that everyone who had contributed to this gift had done so completely voluntarily.

18

Nottingham and Northern Ireland

We very much enjoyed our three week voyage home in the *Empire Fowey*. I was given one month's disembarkation leave, which we spent mostly at Kingsmere.

I visited the War Office and was told that I was on a waiting list for a Grade I Staff appointment, but that it was a long list and so I would be put on the strength of the RA Depot at Woolwich and would be granted unofficial leave. During this period I was called up to Woolwich twice to conduct rather boring Courts of Inquiry. King George VI was due to have dinner at the Officers Mess in November. About a fortnight before the great event, I was summoned to the Garrison Commander's office and told to prepare for the benefit of the senior officers who would be sitting near His Majesty at dinner the answers to any questions H.M. might ask them concerning the silver, portraits, and the furnishing of the dining room in general. This I enjoyed doing very much. I found most of the information I needed in various books in the Mess library, but I also included certain unauthenticated items of interest told me by the excellent Mr Lund, who had been hall porter of the Mess since before the first World War. One item was that the high table at which the King would be sitting had been used during the Crimean War as an operating table! When I delivered my notes to the Garrison Commander, he thanked me for it and I asked him, with tongue in cheek, whether a copy of the questions would be sent to the Palace!

Eventually my Staff appointment came through. I was to be Deputy Assistant Quartermaster General at 5 AA Group at Kimberly, Nottingham. I was most disappointed, and fumed at the treatment I had received from David Lamont and General Evans.

It was a very dreary Headquarters; the GOC was General Norton but the 'live wire' was the Brigadier, General Staff, Brigadier Derek Tullock, who had been Chief of Staff to Orde Wingate during the

Chindit campaign in Burma. The work was very routine and dull.

Joane and I rented a flat in a private house in the Rope Walk near Nottingham Castle, but after a time, as there was no likelihood of us being allotted a married quarter. I bought a small but comfortable house in Stamford Road, West Bridgford.

In November 1951, while Dick was on disembarkation leave, on returning from the Far East where he had been an Air OP Pilot, my mother died, and three weeks later my father died. It was all too depressing. What I would have done if Dick had not been on leave at that time, I really do not know. However, largely thanks to Dick we got through this awful period, disposed of all the effects of our parents, and sold Kingsmere.

Early in 1952, things started to go right for us. The GSO 1 at HQ 5 AA Group was posted away and Derek Tullock persuaded the General to ask for me to be appointed as his successor. General Bob Mathews, who had been GOC Hong Kong before 40 Div. arrived out and whom I knew well, had recently become Military Secretary at the War Office. It was he who ruled that General Evans's recommendation should be expunged and so, at last, I got my Grade I appointment. Then, in June, Michael was born. Nancy Bannerman, her husband Jim having left her to run off with his ATS driver, came and stayed with us for the first month of Michael's life. She was a wonderful help to Joane.

My work of course became more interesting, as I got round the different Brigades and Regiments more frequently. Our Area extended from the Scottish border down the eastern side of the country to Birmingham and East Anglia. One day General Norton and I made an early start to visit our Brigade HQ and Regular Regiment in Newcastle. When we reached the outskirts of Newcastle we saw large numbers of flags all flying at half mast. King George VI had died in the early morning. I attended several AA Practice Camps and was surprised to see what apparent lack of improvement there had been in the accuracy of AA gunnery since 1942, although in these camps they were still firing at towed targets going at the same old speed of about 120 m.p.h., and flying straight courses.

In mid-1953 I was posted to 60 HAA Regiment at Holywood near Belfast as second in command to Lieutenant Colonel Holman, to get my recommendation for Command of a regiment confirmed. After a short period we were allotted a married quarter within Palace Barracks. We all enjoyed the friendly life which existed in a good, well housed Regiment with no shortages of married quarters. It made a perfect setting for Michael's advancement from babyhood to boyhood and for us it had the great benefit of there never being any difficulty finding 'baby sitters'. It was during this period that we saw television for the very first time. The Regiment hired a television set which projected its pictures on to a cinema screen; this was for the coronation of Queen Elizabeth II.

We had a very interesting training season which included going to Practice Camp at Weybourne in Norfolk and also going over to Maryhill Barracks, Glasgow for a short period, before taking part in the big UK manoeuvres.

We had one 'home leave'. Joane, Michael and I crossed from Belfast to Liverpool. We had a rough crossing and Michael in particular found it impossible to sleep; he spent the night reciting nursery rhymes at the top of his voice, and singing. I went on deck next morning to watch our arrival and chatted with a senior staff officer who told me that he had had a miserable crossing, having been kept awake all night by a bloody baby in the next door cabin continuously reciting nursery rhymes! I sympathised with him and ensured that he had disembarked before I allowed the family to come out of my cabin! We hired a car for our leave and did a tour which included a night or two with my Uncle Harry and Aunt Violet at Valelands, Oxted.

The next year I was appointed Camp Commandant of the large TA Training Camp at Barry Budden on the Angus coast for about four months. Captain Griffiths came as my adjutant. I got the local rank of Lieutenant Colonel for this assignment. I soon discovered that the bulk of our work came at weekends, when units departed and others arrived, and that there was very little to do midweek. The Camp was surrounded by three championship golf courses, Carnoustie, Panmure and Monifieth. My adjutant was a keen golfer, so I lost no time in trying to negotiate with the secretary of Panmure a temporary membership for us. He appeared to be strangely unhelpful, turning down my various suggestions, so in the end I said meekly, 'Well, can you suggest anything?' To this, to my astonishment, he answered, 'Yes, you will become honorary members of the club throughout your stay.' He was a charming man and at least once a week he used to take the two of us out to play on other courses! I rented a house at Monifieth and Joane and

Michael occupied it for two months. I bought a very good second hand Standard Vanguard to replace my father's Austin which was getting a bit aged, and we were able to see a good deal of the countryside before returning to Northern Ireland.

On my return I received the wonderful news that I had been appointed to command 246(M) HAA Regiment TA in Londonderry. This was the TA Regiment formed after the war from the Supplementary Reserve Regiment—9 HAA—which I had got to know so well in 1939-40 in Alexandria. Sir Basil McFarland, I was delighted to find, was Honorary Colonel of the Regiment.

Before leaving Belfast we had a very pleasant fortnight's holiday in an isolated cottage on the shore of Lough Swilly. We took my batman Gunner Burton with us to do the chores for us, which included drawing all the water we needed from the local pump. Burton, country born and bred, distinguished himself by going off with a bent pin, a reel of cotton and 'the straightest stick he could find on the mountain' and returning with some quite good sized fish. It amused me greatly because we used often to walk along the beach to the hotel, occupied mostly by anglers, most of whom complained continuously of the lack of fish. I did not dare to tell them of Gunner Burton's success with his crude equipment and a loaf of bread. We thoroughly enjoyed our holiday.

In December we drove up to Londonderry where I received a most enthusiastic reception from Basil and the Territorial Association Secretary, Colonel Harvey. We took over a spacious Victorian house within five minutes walk of the Barracks which was the TA centre. We were provided with a living-in, full time domestic, Rita, who got on with us very well. Colonel Harvey had been one of my Uncle Claude's subalterns before the war.

In England and Scotland by now, TA Regiments consisted of the genuine TA volunteers and ex-National service men who had completed their engagement in the Regular Army and had then to do at least another year with a Territorial Regiment. This we found tended to cause friction in a number of TA Regiments. Ulster had no conscription and so Regiments received no National Service reservists. In other words, every member of the unit was a volunteer. 246 Regiment was, I believe, the Regiment with a greater number of volunteers than any other in the United Kingdom. It was recruited mainly from Londonderry in which there were considerably more Catholics than Protestants. While I was commanding the Regiment, I never experienced a single case of an individual's religion affecting his promotion or popularity, though even at that time one clearly sensed the friction outside the unit. No Catholic, for example, would ever be employed in a local government job. My adjutant was a Catholic as was also one of the Battery Commanders. I suspect that the ratio would have worked out at about 60% Protestant—40% Catholic, but there was no need for statistics!

Soon after I took over command, a Regular WO Class I was posted to us as Regimental Sergeant Major; he proved to have been a Gunner in my section in P Battery in Catterick; we had both been members of the Battery Football eleven. He had grown to become a very impressive Warrant Officer, and quickly became a very highly respected RSM; I was lucky.

It was a curious life. There was a small cadre of civilians or regulars to maintain the guns, equipment, and vehicles, and to keep the Barracks ticking over. There were two drill nights each week and weekend training every week. These training sessions were well attended. There were plenty of social occasions organised by the Regiment. We had very good liaison with the local weekly paper and our activities were well covered in it.

As I was the most senior Army officer north of Belfast, I was always called in by the Mayor to attend civic functions, and such occasions as being on hand when distinguished visitors called to sign the Mayor's book.

The local foxhounds were the Strabane Hunt; their country was half in Ulster and half in Eire. During what was left of the hunting season I had about a dozen days out with the Hunt, all on horses lent to me for the day by kind members. It was great fun. The Master looked very like Mr Pickwick and, not being a great horseman, was frequently in trouble. On the second day I was out, we came across a wide stone wall, about four feet high. Some horses 'flew' it, i.e. jumped it clear, others 'banked' it, i.e. jumped onto it and off it without out a pause. The poor Master's horse jumped on to it and stopped on top, the horse walking along the top of the wall. Members of the field pushed the horse as hard as they could, while the Master was beating it and giving forth good Irish oaths. The horse occasionally reared on its hind legs, only to do an about turn and walk along the top of the wall in the other direction! It was a wonderful scene and could have happened nowhere else than in Ireland. I soon discovered that it did not pay to take one's own line across country as there was a lot of bog which was far from easy to recognise. It was all most friendly and enjoyable.

On several days when I was out with them, Princess Alexandra (the Queen's cousin, daughter of the Duke of Kent and Princess Marina) was also one of the Field. She was accompanied by a police jeep and a mounted member of the Royal Ulster Constabulary, part of whose job was to stop the Princess from straying into Eire. The border was not clearly defined and the Princess had great amusement in giving her escort the slip and following the hounds into the Free State.

Sadly, after I had commanded the Regiment for just over six months, there was a big reorganisation of the Territorial Army which among other things made drastic cuts in AntiAircraft Regiments. Poor 246 Regiment was ordered to disband and become part of another Regiment based on Coleraine. It was a bitter blow to the Regiment and also to me as, having had less than a year in command, I could give up all idea of any further promotion.

I received a posting to HQ Western command as GSO 1 (Physical Training) at Chester. We were very sorry to have to leave Ireland. Rita decided to accompany us to Chester.

19

Chester 1955—1958

The offices of HQ Western Command were in Chester Castle, where the officers Mess was also located. We were allotted a very nice married quarter in Horrocks Road on the outskirts of the city. It was in a secluded cul-de-sac and contained a dozen or more Field Officers' married quarters which all faced onto a recreation ground; on the other side of the ground was a kindergarten school called 'The Firs'. Michael had any number of friends to play with in safety, and eventually started his schooling at 'The Firs'. Baby-sitting was no problem by day and if Joane and I wanted to go out to dinner or to a dance, I could always get one of the clerks to spend the night with us and look after Michael until we returned. Rita only stayed for six months before returning to Londonderry.

I enjoyed my job. I was responsible for the Physical Training throughout Western Command, from Carlisle in the north through the whole of Wales and as far south as Herefordshire. I was also responsible for all the War Department sports grounds, stadia and gymnasia, and for the Command Physical Training School which together with most of the Gunner Training Regiments was in Oswestry. I had a 'Master-at-Arms' (a commissioned APTC Instructor) to help me. He was a wonderful help in running such events as the Command Athletics Meeting, Boxing and Swimming Championships. I also had a retired officer who controlled the training grant and sports grounds.

We bought a caravan soon after we arrived and made good use of it, towed behind our Vanguard, for holidays. These included a holiday in Anglesey, and a tour visiting relations and friends during which we used the caravan for bed and breakfast while spending the rest of the days with our hosts. We also used it for attending the Badminton Horse Trials.

I was much honoured to be asked to be a member of the Army Cricket Selection Committee, which gave me great pleasure and brought me into contact with a younger generation of cricketers, including Peter Richardson (Kent), John Edrich (Surrey), Philip Sharp (Yorkshire) and Alan Jones (Glamorgan), all of whom played for England.

At the start of each cricket season I ran a cricket coaching course at the Command PT School to which units were very co-operative in sending such talented cricketers as they had. I selected a Gunner Lenham to help me run the courses; he played subsequently for Sussex for many years, finally becoming the Sussex coach. His son, as I write, has just returned from captaining an England Under-18 eleven in the West Indies. To enable me to run these courses, I attended a MCC coaching course at Lilleshall, run by my ex-housemaster Harry Altham. It was great to see him again, and looking just the same as he had done twenty-five years previously. I captained the Western Command eleven in all the Non-Representative matches, the ones against Malvern and Shrewsbury and a most enjoyable one against General Sir Oliver Leese's XI, in which he always included a number of county players.

The C-in-C Western Command, for most of the time that I was there, was General 'Bolo' Whistler, who was a very fine man and a keen sportsman; his Brigadier General Staff was an Old Wykehamist, Brigadier Willie Turner, with whom I got on very well.

As my three-year appointment was nearing its end, I made the decision to apply for early retirement—the Golden Bowler, it was called. The Gunners particularly had far more substantive Lieutenant Colonels than they could employ and I realised that if I stayed on to my retirement age I would just have uninteresting extra-Regimental dull jobs. So I sent myself on a Football Coaches course at the Command School and started advertising myself for employment as a sports master, capable of teaching mathematics, at a preparatory school. I was very surprised at the number of letters I received from headmasters asking me to visit them for an interview. So, for my 'retirement leave' we piled into the car and trailer and headed south. The first school I visited was an excellent one near Henley. I was offered the job but rather regretfully I turned it down for two reasons. Firstly the difficulty of finding a house for a reasonable price in that very expensive area, and secondly that I would have been taking over from a very renowned man who had a house close to the school which he was going to keep for life. He was

R.C. (Tishy) Robertson-Glasgow and I knew him as a County cricketer and a most amusing writer. Then on we went to St Leonards. Hilary Barber, who had recently taken over the school—Summer Fields—from his father who had had it while I was at Sandrock Hall, invited the three of us to tea. Two hours later I had been offered the ideal job, and had accepted it.

In a way we were all sorry to leave Chester. My job had necessitated my going on frequent tours of inspection. These I had planned with great care; for example my tour which included the Army Apprentices' School at Chepstow, the Gunner Regiment at Crickhowel and the Infantry Depots at Hereford and Brecon I always timed for late October, when the wonderful wooded hills along the Wye valley were displaying the most beautiful autumnal colouring—a most amazing sight. These trips, too, allowed me to keep in touch with many old friends, among them Lionel Lewin and Legs Lyon.

For my 'resettlement' course I elected to go on a course in household maintenance at Catterick. I enjoyed the course very much and a lot of what we were taught proved of value to me when I took over responsibility of the maintenance of the school buildings at Summer Fields. But I cannot say that the course improved my personal efficiency as a 'do-it-yourself' man. However my morale was raised by managing to make, with considerable help from my instructor, a table for our television and the table lamp in the shape of a rustic well which still provides the light for our telephone in the hall.

During August I went to Worcester College, Oxford, to attend a course run by the IAPS (Incorporated Association of Preparatory Schools). The ex-headmaster who was the chief instructor was Pat Knox-Shaw. He was an admirable man. The course was for late entries to the teaching profession in preparatory schools. It lasted a fortnight and was absolutely first class, proving of infinite value to me. We were worked so hard that David Gay, a fellow student and captain of the Army Cricket eleven and I realised that the only chance of having game of golf during the fortnight was to tee off at 7 a.m. on the Sunday morning. This we did with special permission of the Secretary of Frilford Heath. We were back in time to attend morning chapel!

20

Summer Fields 1958—1966

We bought High Dene, a very nice house overlooking Linton Gardens and within ten minutes walk of Summer Fields. The garden was rather bigger than we would have liked, but we were able to keep the gardener and so we lived very comfortably.

I started work at Summer Fields in September 1958. I was given two mathematics classes, one being the one which introduced the boys to algebra and geometry, the other being the bottom form but one. Reluctantly I had to agree to taking a junior French form, on being assured that the present and imperative tenses were the only ones I would have to teach! and a middle of the school English and Geography. I also took over the first eleven football and the Physical Training. It was by no means a dull life!

Our first football match was against Hurst Court on their ground, which was very much larger than ours and less well mown. I was told that we had not won against them since before the war. Fortunately we had two very fast runners in our forward line, so my instructions to the halves and inside forwards was to kick the ball as hard as they could to the right hand corner flag, where hopefully our outside right would reach it before their left back. He was then to centre it and our centre forward would put the ball in the net. This happened exactly as planned in the first ten minutes of the game, which we won 1-0. I must admit that what made my day was that our outside right was Viscount Raynham and our centre forward was Baron Bonde! The next day a telegram arrived from Pat Knox-Shaw congratulating me on beating Hurst Court! What a man! Fancy anyone taking the trouble of finding out the result of such a match and then bothering to send a congratulatory telegram. He was someone very special.

At the end of my first term, assessing my performance, I thought that I had done well in teaching mathematics. My success with the lower form I put down to my adoption of a tip given to us on the

Oxford course, which was occasionally to have a test of 'tables' on the lines of Bingo. I started each lesson with a game of Bingo, by public acclaim, awarding a Mars bar to the winner. It was remarkable how quickly their knowledge of all the tables, and their mental arithmetic, improved! The questions varied from 'what is 12 x 11?' to 'how many furlongs are there in eight miles?' I was reasonably happy with my junior French class and the geography, but uneasy over the English class. Football and PT had gone very well and the boys were most encouraging in telling me how very much more they had enjoyed those activities than previously, so when I received a very long letter from Hilary Barber I was very worried. The gist of his letter was that on medical advice he felt that he must give up the headmastership at the end of the next term. Both he and his father would like me to take over from him before the start of the summer term. I was aghast, and after discussing it with Joane I wrote back that I would be quite prepared to take over for two terms if that would give him sufficient time to get himself fit enough to continue, but that I thought that it would be very bad for the school if an unqualified and inexperienced man was appointed. His answer was that he had to give up for good at the end of term. So with some regrets I turned his offer down.

When the next term started it was agreed that 'Ran' Ogston, a great friend of Hilary's since University days, and who had been teaching at Summer Fields for seven years, and I should become joint headmasters. Ran was unmarried, so obviously this arrangement would involve Joane in a considerable amount of work. Bless her, she agreed to do her share. We really made a pretty good team. Ran's special responsibilities were syllabi, work programmes and discipline. Mine were accounting, maintenance of the buildings and grounds, and all games and sports. We shared responsibility in choice of teaching staff and boys' entries. Joane of course had to do correspondence with parents concerning boys' illness, and also engaged and supervised domestic staff.

Things inevitably went wrong to start with. We had to replace an assistant cook, so we put an advertisement in the local paper, forgetting that the paper was published on the Saturday, which happened to be our sports day. Joane was told that there was a lady to see her. She put her in the drawing room and for a long time could not decide whether she was a mother of one of the boys or whether she was another cook applying for the job. All was well.

Summer Fields 1960
Seated in the middle left to right:-
Mrs Joane Haig: R.A.L. Ogston: the Author

Joane did not offer her the job, and she turned out to be the mother of one of our senior boys! Parents kept arriving and saying, 'I've come to call for Peter', so we rushed around the class rooms calling, 'Peter, Peter, Peter!' until we found one who was expecting his mother to call for him and checked up that his mother drove the make of car that the lady had come in. It was all very amusing afterwards.

This started eight very happy years. After one term as headmaster, the house in the grounds was completed; we named it 'Meads' and occupied it during the summer holidays. We lived there very happily and very inexpensively for the period which covered Michael's schooling at Sandown, Horris Hill and Winchester. We lived virtually free in Meads and so were able to make the most of the school holidays, once the boys' reports and the bills had been sent out. Each Christmas holidays we had a fortnight's skiing holiday. We went to Klosters and St. Cergue before finally deciding that Wengen was the place for us. Not surprisingly, Michael rapidly became the most proficient skier of the three of us. Joane became the 'Queen of the Nursery slopes'! but was somewhat nervous when on runs which she did not know well. But we all enjoyed our many visits to Switzerland.

I will just generalise over our time at Summer Fields and mention a few of the more amusing episodes.

When we took over we had about eighty boys; after about a year, to keep the fees down, we increased our 'ceiling' to ninety-nine. Our success rate in Common Entrance and scholarship exams maintained the school's high standard. Our teaching staff remained remarkably constant, as did our matrons, outdoor and senior indoor staff.

I took over the Common Entrance maths class as well as my junior class, and kept on my French and geography classes. My biggest boob while teaching French occurred when one day I was called to the telephone for what I knew was bound to be a lengthy conversation, so I told the class to write a few lines, in French of course, about their homes. When I got back, about a quarter of an hour later, one boy held his hand up.

'Please, sir, what is the French for "clean"?'

The word that immediately came into my mind was 'nadif'; a minute later I had serious doubts about my answer! I thought, 'nadif', feminine 'nadive', 'le plus nadif' . . . it all sounded very wrong and to my horror I remembered that 'nadif' was the Arabic for 'clean'. I rushed off to the study; from the dictionary I discovered that 'propre' was what I should have told the boy. I returned quickly and told him that he had better use the word 'propre', and shamelessly added that 'nadif' was a colloquial word used mainly in North Africa.

On the whole, the prep. schools' syllabi had hardly changed at all since my days at Sandrock Hall; neither had Common Entrance papers. We created a science laboratory and taught the top two forms elementary physics and very elementary chemistry. Film strips and recorded BBC material helped considerably.

One day, just before afternoon school, one of our tougher small boys came into the study, where I was working, crying his eyes out. I asked him to tell me his troubles; he blurted out between sobs that his best friend had called his mother 'something worse than sacrilege'.

'What did he call her?' I asked.

More sobs, then, 'Oh, Sir, he called her a prostitute.'

This surprised me, because it was not such a widely known word then as it became a few years later. I tried to comfort him by saying that his best friend could not have known what a horrible name it was to call a lady. I knew his current best friend, so avoided his having to 'sneak' by asking him to send R—— to me. I then sat and wondered how Pat Knox-Shaw or Ken Barber would have dealt with this problem. R—— knocked on the door—a titled boy with blue eyes innocently peeping through his fringe.   I said, 'I hear that you called Mrs M-C a prostitute. Do you know what a horrible name it is to call another boy's mother?'

'Well, no, sir, but I did know that it was pretty hot stuff.'

So I told him that a prostitute was a very low class, common girl, who, to gain money, tempted loving fathers to do things which could cause great trouble and even spoil their marriages. Fortunately he did not want further information, and he went away to apologise to his friend, promising never again to use the offending word. I went into drawing room tea, feeling that I had dealt with a tricky situation rather well. In my geography lesson that followed, the boys were taking it in turn to read aloud out of a textbook about food products. That afternoon the subject had been 'butter'. It ended, rather lamely, 'Sometimes margarine is used as a butter substitute'.

'Who can tell us what "substitute" means?'

A hand waved violently at the back of the class. It was R——.

'Sir, sir, it's a kind of lady . . .'

I stopped him short, before getting the correct answer from another boy. I regretfully realised that my talk with R—— before tea had not been quite the success I had thought it to be!

At games, we had one very serious disadvantage when playing against other schools because Eton, to which most of our boys went, wanted boys as soon as they became twelve years old, whereas other prep schools kept theirs until 13½ or even 14. The difference of eighteen months at that age was very difficult to deal with.

One year when what 12 and 13 year-olds we had were particularly unathletic, I remember a football match when our team consisted of four of our more gifted 11 year-olds and seven others, playing against eleven giants from another school. They were much too fast, too strong and too mature for us. In goal we had Martin Harrison, a very small, very brave boy with a good eye for a ball. He did heroic work behind our clumsy, slow, defence. Just before the final whistle went, Claremont scored their tenth goal. Martin was led off the field weeping and declaring that he had let the school down. The headmaster of Claremont was so impressed however by his performance that the same evening, he sent a huge box of chocolates to our eleven, particularly the goalkeeper, for the way they had fought to the end of the game. The following season we beat them 1-0 and Harrison, playing at inside left, had the pleasure of scoring the winning goal!

The same disavantage applied to cricket. Several times an opposing team arrived with two or more young men, who we hoped to find were junior masters, but who inevitably turned out to be fast bowlers and forceful batsmen; our 11 year-olds, bound for Eton, batted very well but had not sufficient strength to 'pierce the field'. It was very frustrating. However, during my eight years at Summer Fields, five of our boys were capped for Eton, and one for Harrow.

The one happening which gave me the greatest gratification during my time at the school again concerned Martin Harrison. His father had entered him for Radley, into which he should have passed easily, although it was deemed to be only second to Winchester in difficulty. Radley failed him on his Common Entrance results. To recommend a boy too enthusiastically to a public school was a very dangerous thing to do, in case he did not live up to your estimations. So I wrote a long letter to Jack Webster, a housemaster at Harrow, who also ran the cricket there. I had met him while playing in various Free Forester matches during the holidays. I sent it with Martin's Common Entrance papers, extolling his virtues, particularly his guts, ability at games, and his enthusiasm. I also mentioned his one defect—absentmindedness. I quoted the time that he went out to bat, when playing in his first away match for the first eleven, forgetting to take his bat with him, and not realising his error until he tried to take guard! Webster said that he would love to take Harrison, but that he would have to get special permission from the headmaster as his house was already one over strength. It pleased us all greatly when he rang back to say that the headmaster had agreed. In his first year at Harrow, Harrison was in the school boxing team; in his last year, he played the innings at Lords which gave Harrow their first win over Eton for ten years. The Harrovian spectators crowded in front of the pavilion when the match was over, cheering and calling out 'Harrison! Harrison!' until he shyly appeared on the balcony. I felt very privileged to be there.

Playing for Eton in the same match was James Stewart, a less talented cricketer than Harrison, but one who showed tremendous determination to succeed. I certainly gave him far more coaching than I did any other boy. We went down to Winchester to watch 'Eton match'. When we arrived, Eton were batting and Stewart was at the crease. He was eventually out having scored thirty-odd and immediately came to sit with us. I complimented him on his strokes to balls on or just outside his leg stump. He said that he too was pleased with them 'because I had not been doing them well all season. But when I saw your car drive into the field, I remembered what you had told me, and it all became easy.'

When I became a headmaster I bought a large new Jaguar Mark X. Its size became very useful when taking boys on outings. Once I got the whole of our under-eleven football side in for a short journey to another school. Three rode in the boot!

When I joined the school the majority of the boys were the products of immediately post-war marriages. A number of these, unlike mine, proved unsuccessful, so there were a lot of unhappy homes. Most of the boys coped wonderfully well with broken homes, divorces and remarriages. I was however horrified at the end of my first term, when I went to see the boys off on the school train, to find one boy in tears. I asked Hilary Barber about this and he explained how this boy always dreaded going home. His parents were on the verge of ending their marriage, and their only other child was a severely handicapped mongol daughter. Generally speaking, however, we had a splendid lot of boys. There was only one case when we had to ask a parent to withdraw his son, who was a compulsive liar and a bully.

One of our boys was Prince Hassan Bin Talal of Jordan, King Hussein's younger brother—a most likeable character. He innocently caused us a most worrying half hour. One Sunday morning his second brother, the Crown Prince, rang us up to say that he would like to drive down from London and take Hassan out for the day. We agreed and said that we would be in church when he arrived, but that we would arrange for the local detective, who had to accompany Hassan whenever he went out of the school grounds, to be present. We duly arrived back from church, found that Hassan was not in, and assumed that the Crown Prince had collected him and the detective, and had departed. Minutes later, the Crown Prince's car drew up at the front door. Panic! We looked for him in the gym, in the squash court, in the lavatory, in his dormitory. By this time the Crown Prince had downed two cups of coffee and I was wondering how I could confess to him that we had lost his brother! Just then, a police car drove up and out stepped Hassan and his detective. They had miscalculated the Crown Prince's time of arrival and the detective had taken Hassan to the Police Club for a game of snooker!

A year or two later King Hussein who frequently visited us, promoted Hassan over the head of his second brother, to make him the Crown Prince. Hassan eventually went to Harrow where, of all things, he won the school's Shakespeare prize, and became head of his house. His housemaster, whom I met recently, declared that Hassan had proved himself the best disciplinarian he had ever had during his period as housemaster. Soon after Hassan left us, his cousin, son of the previous Queen's brother, joined us as a new boy. Sharif Nasser, his father, very kindly invited Joane, Michael and me to stay in Amman for ten days as his guest. We stayed in the best hotel and every day he arranged visits for us. These included a visit to the palace for an audience with the King, a visit to his farm and racing stable, and visits to Jerash, Petra, Jerusalem and Bethlehem. We all enjoyed it greatly.

The other 'royal' we had was the Crown Prince of Buthan whose father had only a few years to live and whose mother, a most attractive lady, wished him to start his education in England. He brought with him a 'friend' as companion. The friend—Dodo—proved to be a village boy who had never before worn shoes. The Queen could not tell us Dodo's age, but she thought that he was about the same age as Jigme the Crown Prince, who was ten. Jigme spoke some English, but Dodo none at all. They settled in wonderfully well and became very popular with our other boys. We put them both in our under-eleven football eleven with most gratifying results. Largely thanks to Dodo, who wanted to play in bare feet, we won all our under-eleven matches by large margins. The captain of our first eleven, having read in the paper that the Dalai Lama was visiting London, came to see me. He told me that before Jigme and Dodo left Buthan, the Dalai Lama had blessed their football boots. He asked me whether I could arrange for him, while in England, to come and bless our first eleven's boots! I had to disappoint him. At the end of the summer term Jigme and Dodo flew back to Buthan for the holidays and to our sorrow only Jigme returned for subsequent terms. Dodo had, I am afraid, rather outshone Jigme. Jigme was crowned King two years later.

When Ogston and I took over the school we formed it into a charitable trust and appointed our own board of governors. We paid an annual rent to the Barber family. When in 1965 we heard that Hastings Borough Council had decided to compulsorily purchase the whole estate, the negotiations were carried out direct with the Barbers. We, of course, made various suggestions which would enable the school to carry on and, we thought, give the Council sufficient space for building all the Council offices and departments. We offered them the whole of the lower part of the golf course and the whole strip of land fronting the main road. This was refused; they needed the lot and they needed it within four months. In the end, at our behest, they extended this to eight months. This allowed us to give two terms' notice to parents and the staff, which we considered to be the very minimum acceptable. Very sad days followed. In the end, all our boys found other schools. Public schools co-operated by taking boys earlier than booked. Any boys whose parents failed to find places in other prep. schools were accepted by Summer Fields, Oxford, whose staff Ogston joined. One youngest son joined us for our very last term, at the age of six, 'as he had been so looking forward to going to Summer Fields with his elder brothers.'

Joane and I bought Moorings at Cooden Beach for £16,600, which was our dream house. Dorothy Davis, our longest serving domestic, and Arthur Stapley, our groundsman, both agreed to come once or twice a week to help us.

We had had eight most happy years at Summer Fields, and I felt that they had been most rewarding ones. Looking back, I think that the sudden loss of the school came at the right time for our family. I could have been tempted to stay there too long, which would not have been fair to Joane, and we would never have acquired Moorings.

I had continued to play cricket in the holidays, mostly for the Sussex Martlets, and occasionally for the Free Foresters and I Zingari. My last match was for the MCC—the eleven included the great Denis Compton, Fellows-Smith (South Africa) and Dr Clark (West Indies).

Moorings, 1966—

I was in my fifty-fifth year when we settled into this lovely house with its incredible views of the sea and across the bay to Beachy head, too young really to retire completely. We were however very well off financially. From the time in 1938 when I joined the British Military Mission, till the time I was married in 1945, all my Army pay had gone straight into the bank, and the manager had bought Victory Bonds and other government securities for me. These, plus legacies from my mother and my father, and from Joane's father and her brother Byam, together with our cheap living at Meads, meant that we had built up a very satisfactory financial position.

Our trips to Wengen continued. After Michael left Winchester, Joane and I continued these trips. We gradually found ourselves doing more curling than skiing.

We took two trips on P & O's *Canberra*, round the world in 1975 and 1977 respectively. We had previously done a cruise on the *Andes* to Las Palmas and the West Indies which convinced us that we loved the life on a cruise ship.

Since then we have spent most enjoyable and quite successful golfing holidays at Marbella in Spain's Costa del Sol where eventually we bought a time-share villa on the lovely Aloha golf course for two weeks each year in January and February. During these holidays Joane has won several golf prizes and I won one or two, including a £240 electric organ which gave us a lot of fun.

During my long and happy retirement, I have never found myself getting bored. I only once accepted a paid job. This was when Jack Hawkins, who had a thriving rope factory in Hailsham, invited me to join his staff to write out training schemes for teaching new employees the skills required for operating the different machines used in making ropes from multiplait hawsers to yachting cords. These schemes were needed, frankly, more for obtaining a large grant from the Wool Training Board rather than for making

a dramatic improvement in the efficiency of the Company's training. I was paid by the hour, and put in about ten hours work a week.
It also involved me in trips to Leeds to liaise with the Training
Board, and to Glasgow to visit Hawkins and Tipson's other major
factory. I did this for about a year and duly earned the company the
maximum training grant. I heard later that the Training Board sent
some of my training schemes to other rope makers, as an example
of what was required! Jack Hawkins wanted me to stay on, to see
how it all worked out. But I knew in my heart of hearts that it was
largely irrelevant and that very soon training would revert to the
age-old system of 'sitting by Nellie' (the Wool Training Board's
term).

I became honorary treasurer of the Bexhill residents' Sea
Defences Association. This we formed when in 1974 erosion of the
coastline became severe after poorly constructed groynes were
swept away by a very severe gale.

I shall not go into details of the interminable struggle we had
with Rother District Council, first to make them take any action at
all, and subsequently to stop them over-reacting. Under the guise of
securing the shore line they put up a plan that included building a
concrete roadway behind the sea wall all the way from Bexhill to
Cooden Beach. Under this scheme they wanted among other
things to compulsorily purchase a large slice of our front lawn to
make an access road down to the proposed roadway and of course
to purchase, in the same way, from all owners of properties extend-
ing to the beach, a wide strip to build a splash wall and the concrete
roadway. After two years of argument there was a Ministry of the
Environment Inquiry held in Bexhill, which eventually ruled in
our favour.

I became Honorary Secretary of the IAPS Golf Society. My main
duty was to organise the Annual Golf Meeting during the Easter
holidays, for preparatory school headmasters. This I did for about
ten years. I also organised golf teams for various matches for the
Royal Artillery, the Senior Golfers Society, to which I was elected
in 1970, and the Sussex Martlets. I was also elected Captain of the
RA Golfing Society in 1984. I played regularly in their spring and
autumn meetings, mostly with my old friend from our days in
Cairo, Colonel 'Tiny' Shorland.

Both Joane and I still play a great deal of golf and still enjoy it
greatly even though we do not hit the ball as far as we used to. In

1975 Joane, to my surprise, suddenly announced that she would like to learn to play bridge. I was delighted with her decision. Since then, we have very much enjoyed family bridge parties and have occasionally played in various bridge tournaments at Cooden Beach Golf Club, even coping with the occasional duplicate bridge tourney.

I should have mentioned that Joane and I both became members of Rye Golf Club in 1966. I have made many good friends there and very much enjoy the whole atmosphere of the club and the excellence of the golf course. I also appreciate the excellent lunches they serve.

Television watching has inevitably taken up perhaps too much of our time, but it has given us endless enjoyment. What with that, gardening and mowing the lawns, golf and bridge and our extravagant holidays, there are very few dull moments.

Michael, Valerie, and our grandchildren Jonathan and Stephanie come and visit us regularly, and we go up to them for special occasions. We get great pleasure in watching their personalities and careers develop.